# Unitarians: Together in Diversity

A Survey of the Beliefs, Values, and Practices of Contemporary British Unitarians

Compiled by Sue Woolley

The Lindsey Press
www.unitarian.org.uk/pages/unitarian-books

Published by the Lindsey Press
on behalf of the General Assembly of Unitarian
and Free Christian Churches
Essex Hall, 1–6 Essex Street, London WC2R 3HY, UK

© The General Assembly of Unitarian and Free Christian Churches 2018

ISBN 978-0-85319-090-5

All rights reserved. No part of this publication may be reproduced, stored in a retrieval system, or transmitted, in any form or by any means, electronic, mechanical, photocopying, recording or otherwise, without the prior permission of the publisher.

Designed and typeset by Garth Stewart, London
Front cover image by David Chidgey, artglassmosaics.com

Printed and bound in the United Kingdom by
Lightning Source, Milton Keynes

## UNITARIANS

*we are the community of the welcoming smile
we are the community of the proffered hand
we are a household of religious belonging
we are a church of spiritual searchers
we are a church of friendly debaters
we are a church concerned with worship
our saints are Humility, Honest Good Faith,
Openness, Freedom, Compassion
and whatever we lack
may be in the backpack
of the next pilgrim willing to join us ...*

Joe Hooper, November 2017

# Contents

| | | |
|---|---|---|
| Introduction: | A faith without a creed | 1 |
| Chapter 1 | The survey respondents: some data | 6 |
| Chapter 2 | The meaning of 'Unitarian'; the roles of freedom, reason, and tolerance | 20 |
| Chapter 3 | Religious authority; Unitarian ritual and liturgy | 36 |
| Chapter 4 | Unitarian views on morality; sexuality, gender, and marriage; inclusion and equality | 51 |
| Chapter 5 | Religion and politics; Earth and the environment; war and peace; and social justice issues | 67 |
| Chapter 6 | Unitarian perspectives on divinity | 84 |
| Chapter 7 | Unitarians' relationship with Christianity | 95 |
| Chapter 8 | Unitarians and Christian festivals | 110 |
| Chapter 9 | Unitarians' relationship with other faith traditions | 124 |
| Chapter 10 | Unitarian views on evil, sin, and personal salvation | 135 |
| Chapter 11 | Unitarians and mysteries beyond reason | 149 |
| Chapter 12 | Unitarian spiritual practices and activities | 163 |
| Chapter 13 | What holds British Unitarians together in the twenty-first century? | 181 |
| Recommendations for further reading | | 185 |
| Acknowledgements | | 188 |
| About the author | | 189 |

# List of figures

| | | |
|---|---|---|
| Figure 1.1: | Ages of Respondents | 7 |
| Figure 1.2: | Unitarian General Assembly Congregational Survey 2013: Ages | 8 |
| Figure 1.3: | Gender Identification of Respondents | 9 |
| Figure 1.4: | Unitarian General Assembly Congregational Survey 2013: Gender Identification | 9 |
| Figure 1.5: | Geographical Location of Respondents | 10 |
| Figure 1.6: | Number of Congregations in each Region | 11 |
| Figure 1.7: | How Respondents learned about the Unitarian movement (from options supplied) | 12 |
| Figure 1.8: | How Respondents learned about the Unitarian movement (other options) | 13 |
| Figure 1.9: | Respondents' position on the Unitarian spectrum (from options supplied) | 14 |
| Figure 1.10: | Individual perspectives on position on the Unitarian spectrum | 15 |
| Figure 1.11: | Respondents' involvement with the Unitarian community (from options supplied) | 17 |
| Figure 2.1: | How the word 'Unitarian' is defined (from options supplied) | 21 |
| Figure 2.2: | Views about Freedom of Religious Belief (from options supplied) | 26 |
| Figure 2.3: | Views about the Role of Reason in Faith/Spirituality (from options supplied) | 29 |
| Figure 2.4: | Views about the Meaning of Tolerance (from options supplied) | 32 |
| Figure 3.1: | Sources of Religious Authority (from options supplied) | 38 |
| Figure 3.2: | Views on the use of ritual / liturgy (from options supplied) | 40 |

| Figure 3.3: | Unitarian Rituals experienced by Respondents (from options supplied) | 44 |
| --- | --- | --- |
| Figure 3.4: | Respondents' Responses to some common Unitarian Rituals | 45 |
| Figure 4.1: | Views on Morality (from options supplied) | 52 |
| Figure 4.2: | Views on Gender, Sexuality & Marriage (from options supplied) | 57 |
| Figure 4.3: | Views on Inclusion and Equality (from options supplied) | 62 |
| Figure 5.1: | Views on Religion and Politics (from options supplied) | 68 |
| Figure 5.2: | Views on the Earth and the environment (from options supplied) | 72 |
| Figure 5.3: | Views on War and Peace (from options supplied) | 76 |
| Figure 5.4: | Views on social justice issues (from options supplied) | 80 |
| Figure 7.1: | Beliefs about Jesus (from options supplied) | 96 |
| Figure 7.2: | Beliefs about the Holy Spirit (from options supplied) | 99 |
| Figure 7.3: | Views on the Trinity (from options supplied) | 103 |
| Figure 7.4: | Views about the Bible (from options supplied) | 105 |
| Figure 8.1: | The Significance of Christian Festivals for Respondents (from options supplied) | 111 |
| Figure 9.1: | Other Faith Traditions important to Respondents (from options supplied) | 125 |
| Figure 9.2: | The important aspects of other Faith Traditions (from options supplied) | 127 |
| Figure 12.1: | Religious, Spiritual, Both or Neither | 164 |
| Figure 12.2: | The Importance of Spiritual / Devotional Practices to Respondents (from options supplied) | 174 |
| Figure 12.3: | Respondents' Participation in Unitarian Activities (from options supplied) | 176 |
| Figure 12.4: | Respondents' Membership of Unitarian Societies (from options supplied) | 177 |

# *Introduction*
# *A faith without a creed*

Dating back 450 years and still evolving, Unitarianism is a faith which imposes no creed or dogma on its followers. It is an inclusive religious and spiritual movement, founded in the Judaeo-Christian tradition but now much broader than that. It is a different way of approaching life and religion, based on an appeal to reason, conscience, and the individual's own life experience, rather than adherence to a set of prescribed beliefs and practices: it is a "faith without a creed".

Unitarians form a religious and spiritual community in which each person can explore what gives his or her life meaning and purpose. Each Unitarian congregation, and each Unitarian society, and the movement nationally – known in Great Britain as the General Assembly of Unitarian and Free Christian Churches – is a faith community made up of individuals on a spiritual journey who have come together because they share an open and inclusive attitude to religion and spirituality.

Unitarians affirm for each individual the right of private judgement in matters of religion and spirituality: no-one should be under any pressure to sign up to particular beliefs. In practice, many Unitarians *do* hold many beliefs in common; but this is not a prerequisite for being a member of the Unitarian community. Unitarians are free to treat new ideas critically and take from them what speaks to their own reason and conscience, and what makes sense in the context of their own life experience, in order to live their life in the best and truest way they can. The sole proviso is that any belief that excludes, harms, or belittles another person or group will not be endorsed by a Unitarian community.

It is also important to recognise that Unitarian beliefs change over time. Unlike most mainstream Christian denominations, Unitarians recognise that, as people have new experiences and encounter new ideas, their beliefs may change. The beliefs of most long-term Unitarians will evolve over the years, according to what they see and hear and learn and experience and take to heart. They find this liberating.

So Unitarianism is a continually evolving faith. This book is a summary of the findings of a survey of contemporary Unitarians in Great Britain, conducted in the Spring of 2017; as such, it can present only a snapshot, not a definitive credo. Its purpose was to discover the range and depth of present-day Unitarian and Free Christian beliefs, values, and spiritual practices and activities; and, in doing so, to better understand what it is that holds Unitarians "together in diversity". It is the outcome of a project by one Unitarian to start a conversation with other Unitarians, to establish whether there can be a meeting of minds and hearts amid the many and diverse beliefs and practices which make up the Unitarian movement in Great Britain today.

Within the Unitarian movement, one of the most consistent concerns is how little is known about it by outsiders. The challenge of communicating the Unitarian faith is a considerable one, to some extent due to the diversity of opinion among its members. It seems to be easier for most Unitarians to communicate what they *don't* believe or subscribe to, rather than to positively affirm what they *do*. This project attempts to discover what contemporary British Unitarians *do* believe, and how they live out their beliefs, both within their congregations and societies, and in their daily lives.

The first step was to formulate a questionnaire. It was divided into eight sections:

- information about respondents (to give a context for the responses)
- attitudes to the basic tenets of Unitarianism
- views on the Unitarian ethos and values
- beliefs about the Divine
- Unitarians' relationships with Christianity
- Unitarians' relationships with other faiths
- beliefs about certain theological and spiritual concepts
- Unitarian spirituality and activities.

The first draft of the questionnaire was circulated to five ministerial colleagues. Discussion within this group resulted in amendments and further drafts, until a final text was agreed.

The questions were partly based[1] on those in Cliff Reed's book, *Unitarian? What's That?*,[2] but it was necessary to address Unitarian spirituality and activities in greater detail. In general, multiple-choice questions were used; but because these were personal questions, the choices were made as open as possible. Of course, not all answers could be anticipated, and so an 'Other' section was included for each question, for those who did not see their own beliefs or positions represented in the options offered. This has made the analysis more complicated, but it was necessary, due to the personal nature of religious and spiritual beliefs, and to the fact that discovering the *diversity* of beliefs within the denomination, as well as finding out what Unitarians have in common, was a key objective of the project.

The use of both quantitative and qualitative analysis was important. When respondents chose two or more of the given options, it was not possible to know whether each option had equal weight for them, or whether some were of greater significance. Encouraging respondents to write more freely about their responses allowed for more nuanced viewpoints and development of the quantitative data. The qualitative analysis was done by a detailed analysis of the comments, looking for common threads of belief or viewpoint. The quotes selected from the comments are ones deemed to be representative of each particular thread.

Compiling a questionnaire is a creative act. It is never complete, and never perfect, although these are of course the aims. This questionnaire has seemed to work reasonably well, although in retrospect it is recognised that small changes could have been made to clarify meaning at certain points (noted in the text).

---

1  Particularly those in the 3rd, 4th, 5th, 6th and 7th sections of the survey.
2  Cliff Reed, *Unitarian? What's That?: Questions and Answers about a Liberal Religious Alternative* (Lindsey Press, London, 1999; latest edition 2018).

The primary concern was to be inclusive and attract responses from a wide cross-section of Unitarians across Great Britain. To that end, information was sent out to all District Associations and to every congregation; to all Ministers and Lay Pastors on the General Assembly Roll; to all Lay People in Charge; to all members of the Unitarian Association for Lay Ministry; and to all students on the Worship Studies Course. Details were also published on the UK Unitarians Facebook page, and in the national Unitarian press. The staff at Essex Hall, the Unitarian headquarters in London, included it in a national mailing, and copies were made available at the 2017 General Assembly meetings. Younger people were contacted through the GA Youth Officer.

The initial response was encouraging: eventually 377 questionnaires were sent out, and 257 were returned: a response rate of 68 per cent. Absolute anonymity was guaranteed, with no names attached to any comments that might be shared with others. But even with the good number of responses, the analysis which follows represents only the beliefs of those who completed the survey – a self-selected group, who are likely to be people who are more than usually active within the movement. It is acknowledged that the findings reported in this book have emerged from a very particular Unitarian pool, rather than representing the beliefs of all British Unitarians.

The final version of the survey contained 41 questions; these questions and the options offered to participants are repeated in the text at the point where the data and comments from the survey are presented. The chapter order follows the order of the questions in the survey. Each chapter considers a number of questions, firstly looking at the choices made by respondents from the options supplied, and then sharing some representative comments made by them. At the end of each chapter there is a summary of the findings, followed by a series of questions for further thought. These may be used for self-reflection, or as part of a study-group programme.

The final chapter draws on the preceding chapters to consider to what extent there is commonality of view, approach, and attitude, and whether this might point to at least a partial definition of what it means to be a Unitarian in Great Britain today. The key finding of the study is that Unitarians and Free Christians are both spiritually and theologically diverse. This could be a strength, rather than a weakness, if there is agreement and togetherness on the principles that underpin the spiritual journey. Furthermore there is a need to foster communities where all are welcome, even while dissenting from the particular viewpoints of other members. Where viewpoints appear to be in direct opposition to those of others, then tolerance, mutual respect, and empathy will be necessary for the creation of a safe and loving community.

*Sue Woolley*
*December 2017*

**NOTE:** The abbreviations 'GA' and 'UU' or 'UUA' appeared frequently in respondents' comments. 'GA' means the British Unitarian umbrella body, the General Assembly of Unitarian and Free Christian Churches. 'UUA' means 'Unitarian Universalist Association', the denomination in the United States of America; and 'UU' means 'Unitarian Universalist'.

# Chapter 1
# The survey respondents: some data

*We gather in this meeting house –*
*People of many kinds:*
*Let us, below the surface, seek*
*A meeting of true minds.*

Peter Galbraith, *Hymns for Living*, 172

The latest quota figure for the number of Unitarians in Great Britain (according to the 2016 Annual Report of the General Assembly of Unitarian and Free Christian Churches) was 2,966; but Chief Officer Derek McAuley commented in an article in *The Inquirer* on 24 May 2014: "Other information would however reveal that, if added to the survey results,[3] the Unitarian community is much bigger than the quota number. ... We are probably talking about between 4,500 and 5,000 as the true size of our wider Unitarian community."[4] So, depending on which figure one adopts, the 257 respondents in this survey represent between 5 and 8.5 per cent of Unitarians in Great Britain. But are they representative of the movement as a whole?

The first section of the questionnaire was designed to elicit some basic facts about the 257 respondents. Participants were asked the following questions:

---

3   See Figures 1.2 and 1.4 below.
4   Derek McAuley, "Reports of death may be exaggerated", *The Inquirer*, no. 7843, 24 May 2014, p.9.

- How old are you?
- Which gender do you identify as?
- Which region of Great Britain do you live in?
- How did you hear about the Unitarian movement?
- Where would you position yourself on the Unitarian spectrum?
- What is your involvement with our Unitarian community?

## *Age and gender identification*

The age breakdown of the respondents is detailed in Figure 1.1. Although the majority of respondents were aged 60 or over, nearly 100 responses (38 per cent) were from people aged between 20 and 59. This corresponds quite closely with the numbers recorded in a survey of Unitarian congregations conducted by the General Assembly in 2013; in that survey, 36 per cent of the 2,205 respondents were aged 64 or younger. If the under-10s in the GA survey are excluded, this percentage falls to 35 per cent. See Figure 1.2.

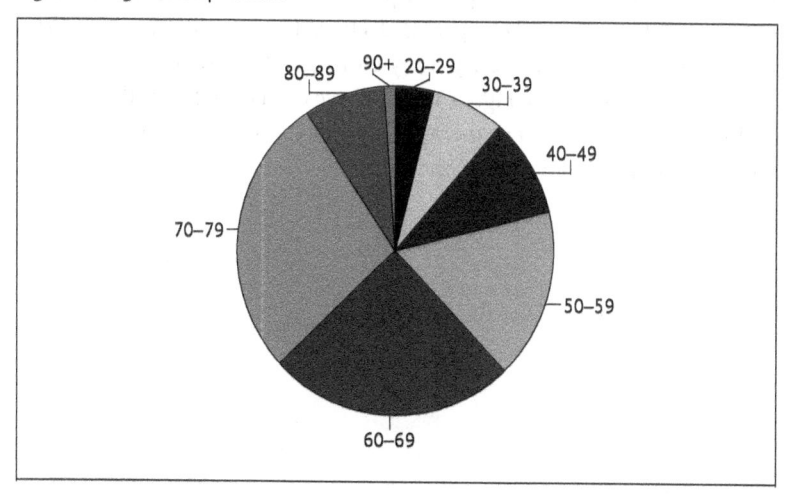

Figure 1.1: Ages of Respondents

*Unitarians: Together in Diversity*

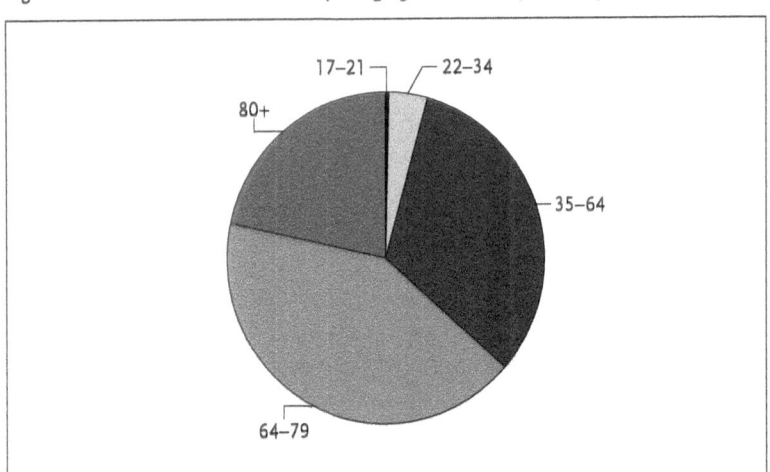

Figure 1.2: Unitarian General Assembly Congregational Survey 2013: Ages

The vast majority of participants in the survey on which this book is based identified as either male (40 per cent) or female (59 per cent). Three identified as "other" – one as "genderqueer", one as "non-conforming", and one as "non-binary" – and one person declined to answer this question. The results are shown in Figure 1.3. They correspond closely to the results of the 2013 GA survey – see Figure 1.4. Thus we can be confident that the age and gender distributions of the 257 participants correspond fairly closely with those of the wider movement.

Figure 1.3: Gender Identification of Respondents

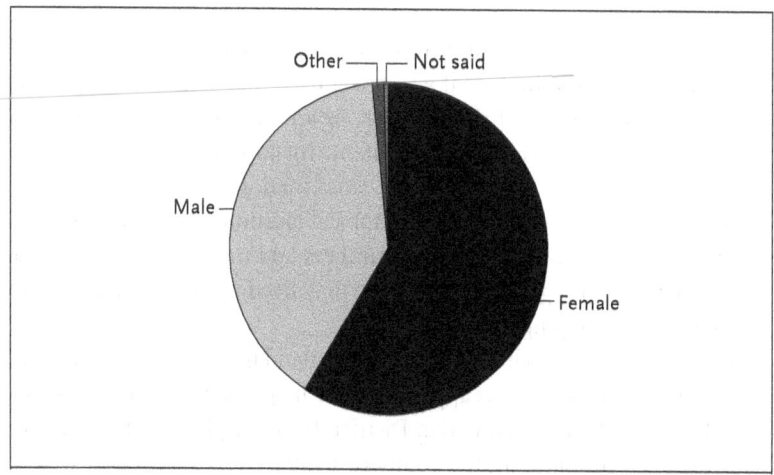

Figure 1.4: Unitarian General Assembly Congregational Survey 2013: Gender Identification

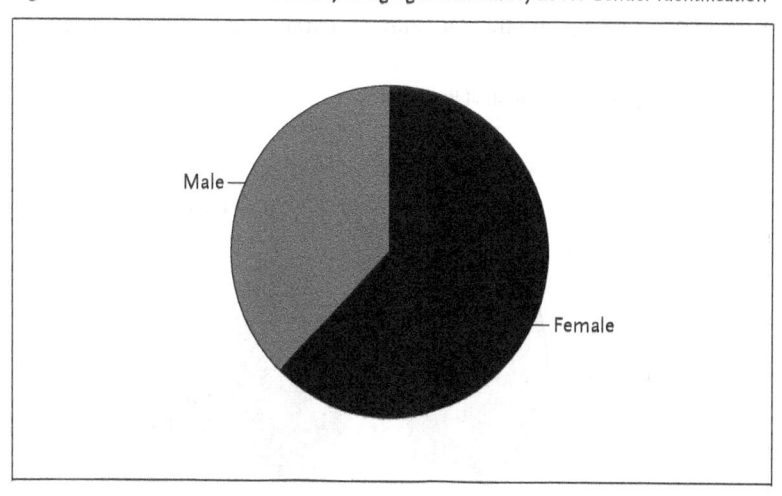

## Where the respondents live

The importance of ensuring a representative geographical spread was understood from the first, as it was recognised that some congregations have a more Unitarian Christian ethos, or a more humanist ethos, than others in different parts of Great Britain. Invitations to respond to the survey were sent out widely (see the Introduction for details), and this policy has been rewarded. The geographical locations of the respondents are detailed in Figure 1.5. (NB: the numbers add up to 258, because one person ticked two regions – one where they lived at present, and one to which they were hoping to return.)

In order to ensure that participants in England ticked the correct region, a list of English counties was appended to each option. Some of the regions included more than one Unitarian District. For example, 'London & South East' included people from the Southern Unitarian Association as well as the London & South Eastern District Provincial Assembly; and 'North East' included people from the Northern Unitarian Association, the Sheffield & District Association, and the Yorkshire Unitarian Union. See Figure 1.5.

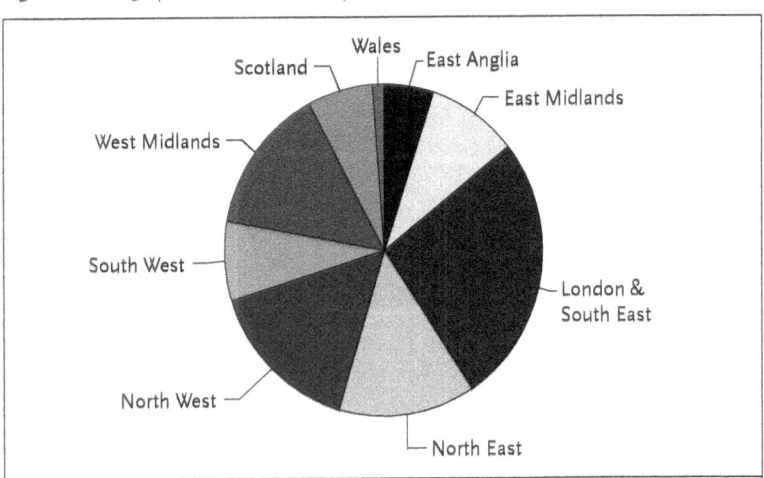

Figure 1.5: Geographical Location of Respondents

The Unitarian General Assembly does not hold equivalent figures. The only possible comparison is with the number of congregations in each region (according to the latest GA Directory) – see Figure 1.6. It is appreciated that this is not comparing like with like, but it may offer some insight.

Figure 1.6: Number of Congregations in each Region

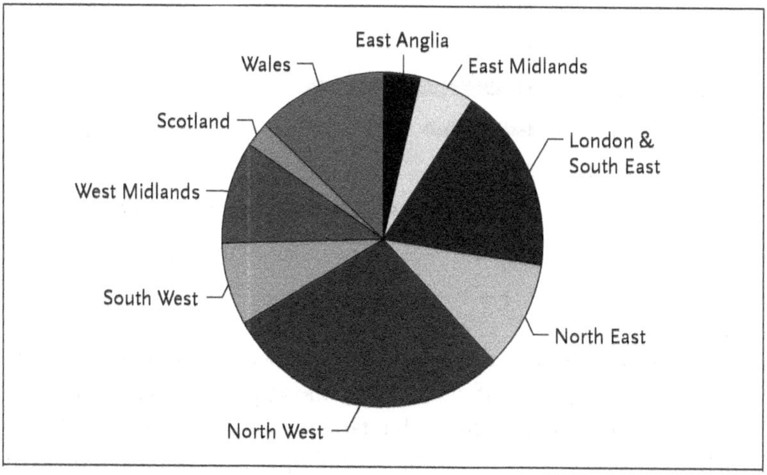

## How respondents learned about the Unitarian movement

While a small number of respondents (37 people, 14 per cent) indicated that they have always been Unitarian, most have become Unitarians later in life. Figure 1.7 shows some of the many ways in which people have come to the Unitarian movement.

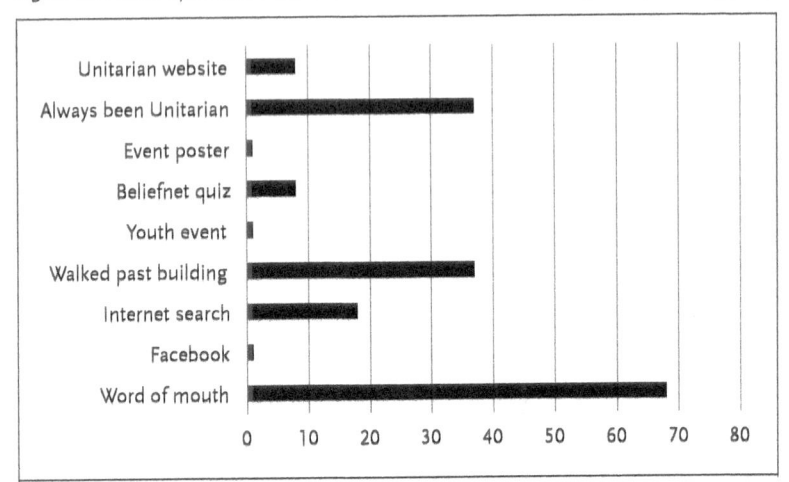

Figure 1.7: How Respondents learned about the Unitarian movement (from options supplied)

| Source | Count |
|---|---|
| Unitarian website | ~8 |
| Always been Unitarian | ~37 |
| Event poster | ~1 |
| Beliefnet quiz | ~8 |
| Youth event | ~1 |
| Walked past building | ~37 |
| Internet search | ~18 |
| Facebook | ~1 |
| Word of mouth | ~68 |

'Word of mouth' was the most common means of introduction into the movement, especially if one includes the 35 people in Figure 1.8 who heard about Unitarianism through a family member or friend, only two of whom also ticked the 'word of mouth' option. This means that 101 respondents (more than 39 per cent) heard about the denomination from other Unitarians directly. Many others were drawn in when walking past a Unitarian building and feeling curious about what might be going on inside. A total of 179 respondents are accounted for in Figure 1.7. The other 78 came to Unitarianism by other routes, most of which are summarised in Figure 1.8. (The figures do not add up to 78, because several people cited more than one of the routes mentioned below.)

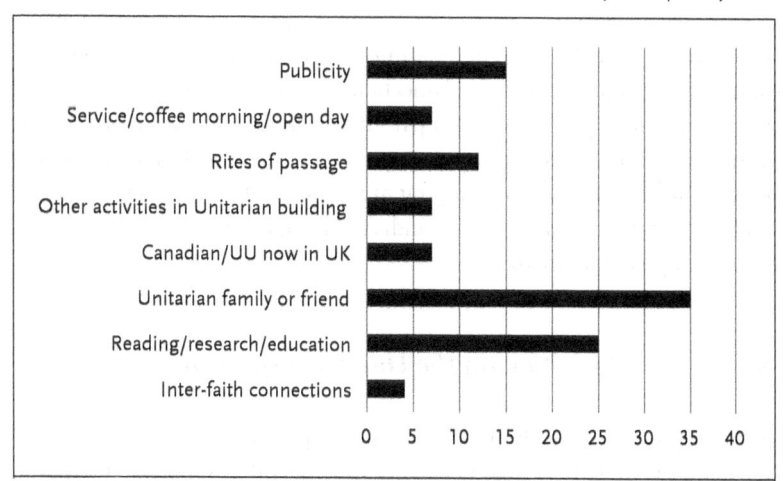

Figure 1.8: How Respondents learned about the Unitarian movement (other options)

| Category | Value |
|---|---|
| Publicity | ~15 |
| Service/coffee morning/open day | ~7 |
| Rites of passage | ~12 |
| Other activities in Unitarian building | ~7 |
| Canadian/UU now in UK | ~7 |
| Unitarian family or friend | ~35 |
| Reading/research/education | ~25 |
| Inter-faith connections | ~4 |

Those finding the denomination through reading, research, or education were mainly either studying religion, or came across Unitarianism through reading or studying history, or, in one case, sociology. One read the memoirs of Christopher Reeve,[5] a couple cited specific Unitarian or Unitarian Universalist books as their route in, and another found it through doing research into their family history.

Those discovering Unitarianism through print media or TV included people who had read advertisements or letters in magazines such as *New Internationalist*, or in the local or national press. One person had read an article by Oxford Unitarian Catherine Robinson in *The Guardian;* one had read a congregational newsletter in a local library; and one saw a piece on a regional news programme, in which a Unitarian minister spoke about dying with dignity.

---

5  The American actor who won a BAFTA award in 1978 for his starring performance in the film *Superman*.

Some of the respondents found Unitarianism because they were specifically looking for a venue for a same-sex marriage ceremony. Others had either attended Unitarian weddings, or married in a Unitarian church, or married a Unitarian. Family connections were many and varied, including having Unitarian parents or grandparents; having an older brother who was a member of a scouting group that met at a Unitarian church; and going to listen to a grand-daughter singing in a choir at Christmas. These routes, and others less easy to categorise, indicate that there are very many ways of discovering Unitarianism.

## *Respondents' position on the Unitarian spectrum*

This was the first question to ask about respondents' religious/spiritual positions. They were invited to tick each category that applied to them; not surprisingly, the options offered did not cover the whole range of Unitarian positions. Figure 1.9 records the options ticked.

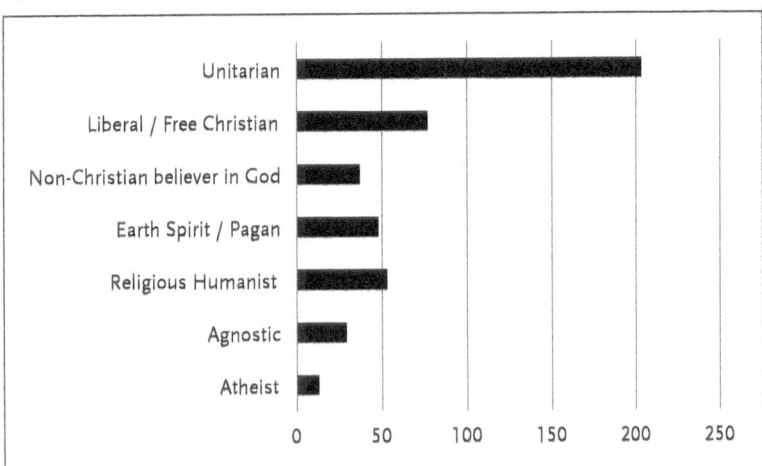

Figure 1.9: Respondents' position on the Unitarian spectrum (from options supplied)

Many of the participants ticking 'Unitarian' ticked another category or categories in addition. Eighty-one people (31 per cent) ticked 'Unitarian' as their only descriptor. Another 122 (47 per cent) ticked one or more of the additional options. The most popular combination was 'Unitarian' + 'Liberal/ Free Christian': 28 (11 per cent). The rest of the responses were many and varied, with some people ticking five or six of the options on offer.

The possibility of combining these options was not adequate for a substantial minority of respondents; they wanted either to qualify their choices or to explain their own unique perspectives. An attempt has been made to summarise these in Figure 1.10.

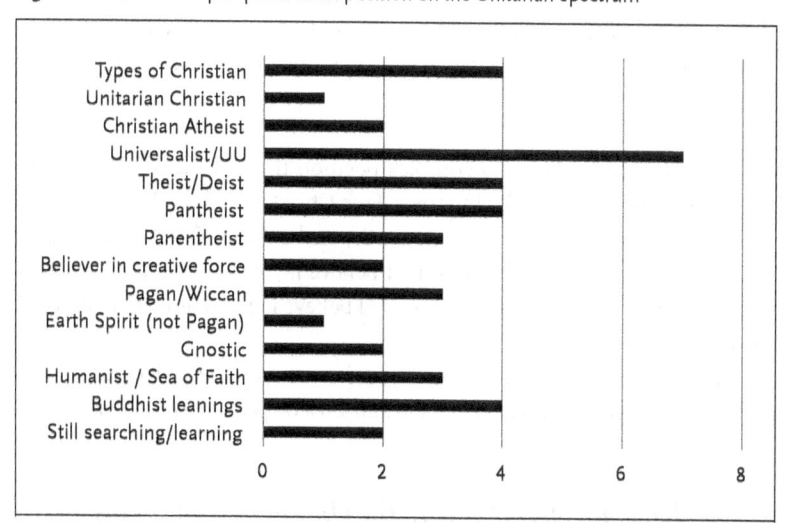

Figure 1.10: Individual perspectives on position on the Unitarian spectrum

| Category | Count |
|---|---|
| Types of Christian | 4 |
| Unitarian Christian | 1 |
| Christian Atheist | 2 |
| Universalist/UU | 7 |
| Theist/Deist | 4 |
| Pantheist | 4 |
| Panentheist | 3 |
| Believer in creative force | 2 |
| Pagan/Wiccan | 3 |
| Earth Spirit (not Pagan) | 1 |
| Gnostic | 2 |
| Humanist / Sea of Faith | 3 |
| Buddhist leanings | 4 |
| Still searching/learning | 2 |

Other positions, which did not fit easily into any category, included Ecumenical Liberal, Spiritualist, Hindu, Pragmatist, Mystic, Creation Spirituality, Teilhardian, Integral Thinker, North American (indigenous) Indian, Qabalist, Empiricist, Process Theologian, and Feminist/ queer. Two people commented that they did not wish to be labelled at all.

### More complex responses

There were several respondents whose positions were more complex and were explained at length. This person ticked the 'Unitarian' box and then wrote:

> *I find even ticking multiple categories doesn't quite hit the button for me. I can find comfort in some aspects of the Earth Spirit tradition. And some days I might feel more agnostic than at other times. I am attracted to what for me is the straightforward nature of religious humanism as exemplified in people I have known who would have described themselves as humanists even though they went to a Unitarian church. I would describe myself as a Unitarian because I believe in the web of interconnectedness: the oneness of the Universe. I find it difficult to conceive of God in terms of a personal deity. But I do believe in a higher intelligence ... that we could call an energy, which is greater than ourselves.*

Another person explained a complex position thus: "None of these quite fits. If I had to, I would tick Unitarian, Free Christian (which I think should be distinguished from Liberal), agnostic, and atheist. But I'm also, in a sense, a traditional Christian, that is, I believe in, and revere, the Christian tradition, which is not the same as saying I believe in the dogma of traditional Christianity."

It is one of the key features of the Unitarian movement that it can welcome and embrace people with such a wide and varied spectrum of beliefs.

### *Respondents' involvement with the Unitarian community*

The aim of the survey was to draw on the widest possible spectrum of opinions, contributed by many different kinds of Unitarian. The question about participants' level of involvement with the Unitarian community was a crucial one. The main options were listed in the questionnaire, but typically the participants had much more to say. They were invited to tick all the categories that applied to them. Figure 1.11 records the results.

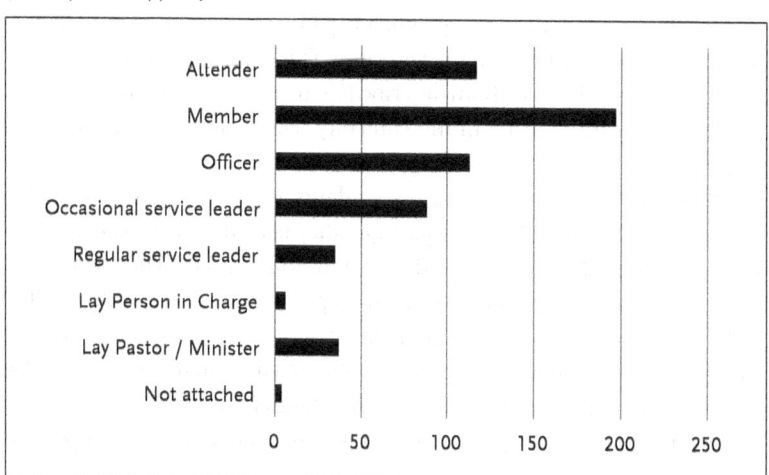

Figure 1.11: Respondents' involvement with the Unitarian community (from options supplied)

[Bar chart showing approximate values:
- Attender: ~115
- Member: ~200
- Officer: ~115
- Occasional service leader: ~90
- Regular service leader: ~35
- Lay Person in Charge: ~5
- Lay Pastor / Minister: ~40
- Not attached: ~5]

It should be noted that the difference between 'Attender' and 'Member' was not sufficiently clear. The aim was to differentiate between casual attenders and committed members, but no fewer than 100 respondents ticked both. Not all congregations define 'attenders' and 'members': an added complication. The number of casual attenders responding is probably very much smaller than indicated.

The vast majority (over three-quarters) of participants were members of a Unitarian community. Eighty-eight (34 per cent) led worship occasionally in their congregations; another 35 (13 per cent) described themselves as 'Regular Service Leaders'; 113 (44 per cent) were also officers in their congregations, and seven more were committee members. Three participants were paid employees of their congregations (not ministers). These figures may suggest that the information on which this analysis is based may be somewhat unrepresentative of the Unitarian community as a whole, as so many of the participants were committed activists. But, as mentioned in the Introduction, the survey pool was self-selected; it was not possible to require less committed Unitarians to participate.

Although only six Lay People in Charge sent in responses, this figure represents 37 per cent of all the LPICs listed in the 2016–2017 GA Directory. Four of the respondents were qualified Lay Preachers on the GA Roll: one-third of the number listed in the Directory. The 37 Lay Pastors or Ministers who responded, eight of whom described themselves as "retired", represent 29 per cent of those listed in the Directory. Three student ministers also responded.

Within their congregations, respondents were very active. They led worship and celebrated rites of passage; they served on committees; they were stewards; they organised flower and coffee rotas. They organised congregational events and projects; they provided the music during the worship services; they looked after the congregation's library; they were custodians of the congregation's history; they led the congregation's Sunday School. Some ran or facilitated 'other than Sunday' groups – engagement groups, meditation groups, discussion groups, bereavement groups, and so on.

In terms of 'outreach' beyond their own congregations, several respondents described ways in which they share their faith. One person commented: "I belong to many religiously orientated discussion groups, and never fail to talk about Unitarianism when the opportunity presents itself." Others were involved in inter-faith work, as we saw in the section above, or represented their congregation or Unitarians on non-Unitarian bodies, such as Churches Together, or the Sea of Faith, and some brought their Unitarian witness to supporting good causes.

It is clear from the foregoing that the respondents to this survey were very much involved in the lives of their congregations, and often in the wider movement. This may mean that their opinions are not entirely representative of all Unitarians in Great Britain. Nevertheless, the chapters which follow present a wide range of beliefs and practices, which demonstrate clearly what a diverse denomination Unitarianism has become.

## *Questions for reflection and group discussion*

1. How did you learn about Unitarianism? And how might we spread the word more widely?

2. Where would you position yourself on the Unitarian spectrum?

3. What do you do to support your Unitarian community? What could you do at District or national level?

# Chapter 2
# *The meaning of 'Unitarian'; the roles of freedom, reason, and tolerance*

*A freedom that reveres the past,*
*But trusts the dawning future more;*
*And bids the soul, in search of truth,*
*Adventure boldly and explore.*

Marion Franklin Ham, *Hymns for Living*, 136

The second section of the survey was entitled 'Beliefs about Unitarianism'. The aim was to elicit views about some basic Unitarian ideas and ways of being. In the first part of this section, respondents were asked the following questions:

- What does the word 'Unitarian' mean to you?
- How would you define freedom of belief?
- What role does reason play in your religious faith/spirituality?
- What does tolerance mean to you as a Unitarian?

### The meaning of the word 'Unitarian'

Participants were offered five options and invited to tick all that applied. There was also a large text box for more discursive replies. The options offered were as follows:

*Chapter 2 The meaning of 'Unitarian'; the roles of freedom, reason, and tolerance*

- It is a free religious faith, without a creed.
- It is an open, inclusive spiritual community.
- It is a Free Christian denomination in which Jesus is revered and followed, but not worshipped.
- It is "the Religion of the Larger Affirmation".[6]
- It is "a movement held together by shared values and a shared approach"[7] to religion and spirituality.

Their responses are detailed in Figure 2.1. Many participants ticked more than one option, the most popular combinations being the following:

- 'Free Religious Faith' + 'Open Spiritual Community' + 'Movement with Shared Values' (22 per cent)
- 'Free Religious Faith' + 'Open Spiritual Community' + 'Free Christian Denomination' + 'Movement with Shared Values' (17 per cent)

Only thirty respondents chose a single option.

Figure 2.1: How the word 'Unitarian' is defined (from options supplied)

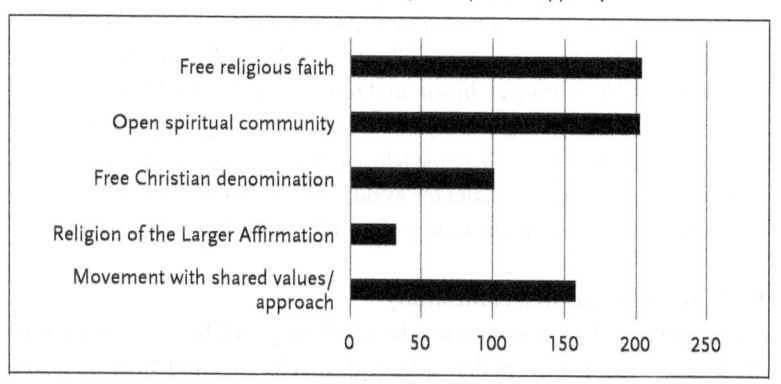

[6] Alfred Hall, *Beliefs of a Unitarian*, 3rd edition, Lindsey Press, 1962, p.7.
[7] Cliff Reed, *Unitarian? What's That?: Questions and Answers About a Liberal Religious Alternative* (Lindsey Press, 1999, latest edition 2018), p.50.

Many respondents made use of the large text box provided, in which to formulate their own definition of what the word 'Unitarian' means. Some commented on particular beliefs which they found central to Unitarianism; others were more interested in how these beliefs work out in practice in Unitarian communities. Their comments are summarised in the shared comments below.

### Free Christian denomination

The respondents who commented further on the 'Free Christian denomination' option were united in their belief that Unitarianism is part of the Protestant Christian tradition and is rooted in Judaeo-Christianity. One wrote: "For me, to really engage with Unitarianism, we must understand its roots in Christianity. Whilst there are Unitarians who do not find their primary spiritual anchor point in Christianity, this need not detract from, or contradict, the fact that Unitarianism has its roots in the Liberal Christian tradition and heritage." Others expressed the importance, to them, of following the teachings of Jesus. Another pointed out:

> *It is a particular religious heritage and religious resource that, in Britain, traces its lineage back to Joseph Priestley and Theophilus Lindsey (with a subsequently strong American influence), and includes our full body of religious ideas, liturgies, hymns and rituals, as well as building on ideas from elsewhere, e.g. Transylvania and Poland. Engaging with this material can be a way of devising religious practices and of helping us to make sense of ourselves and the world, in particular ourselves in the world, with reference to the history of our religious movement.*

### Post-Christian spiritual community

Others perceived the movement to be decidedly post-Christian. One wrote: "It does not stand at the end of a disappearing Protestant Christianity, but at the beginning of a new, more inclusive religious movement which is prepared to redefine the categories in which God and religion are viewed in the modern world." Its openness to a wider variety of spiritual and religious outlooks was perceived as a strength by these participants. Another commented that Unitarians were "on the cutting edge of spirituality in the past – now seeking to be this with a new vision for humanity". Another person extended this idea thus: "It speaks to so many contemporary issues; it does not require a belief in the supernatural; it enables individuals to find their own spiritual path, guided by their own reason, conscience and experience, informed by the insights and wisdom of tradition." Another called it "a religion of grown-ups, or perhaps a grown-up religion".

## The concept of oneness/unity

The concept of oneness or unity was key for some respondents. One wrote: "It's right there in the name: we're united and we're in favour of unity, by which I mean harmony, with everyone and everything on Earth and beyond it." Some, such as this person, also saw it as meaning belief in one God: "There is an overall idea of the power of one-ness, whether it is one God, one people, one planet, one universal home, and the belief that the more we integrate ourselves within a vision of this one-ness, the better existence will be (not just ours, but the life of the planet.)" A few shared the classic definition of Unitarian, as in "It means God is one entity, as opposed to Trinitarian (God as three persons)." One respondent commented in the following terms on what they understood to be the distinctively Unitarian outlook:

> Unitarianism has become a movement which attempts to relate a variety of spiritual outlooks to secular liberalism, with sometimes one and sometimes the other taking precedence. ... While having a high regard for reason, Unitarians recognise it as a fallible instrument and consider that spiritual narratives and artistic expression are at times superior in their insight into the human condition and in their ability to inspire.

## Exploring, inquiring, using reason

Yet others perceived the use of reason to be one of the most important aspects of the movement's distinctive approach to matters of faith and spirituality. One commented: "Unitarianism is an inquiring religious movement for people fascinated with the mysteries of existence and how best to live, and who wish to stand in a good tradition of critical religious exploration and social justice. I think 'reason' is at the core of Unitarianism, as in inquiring, investigating, thinking, and reflecting, and it has always attracted people with active minds and hearts."

### Inclusive, open-minded, valuing diversity

Some were attracted by the fact that Unitarianism is free from dogma: "an all-inclusive creedless religious movement that treats us as mature adults, who have the intelligence, intuition, integrity and sense to make up our own minds about who or how we worship". The fact that Unitarians can learn from other faith traditions, from science, the behavioural sciences, and each other was valued by these respondents.

For some people, it was the journey that mattered: all Unitarians are on a spiritual path, and although the paths may differ, they can travel together, exchanging ideas and insights. One commented: "My belief is that we are all spiritual beings, and that discovering the nature of that spirituality is part of our life's journey."

The open-minded, inclusive approach to matters of religious faith and spirituality and personal identity was highly valued by some. One wrote simply: "It is a religion that accepts you exactly as you are. It is a religion that provides unity in diversity." Another wrote: "It is a community which allows for freedom of thought and belief, and in which it is possible for one's ideas to differ from those of others, without constraint." However, one person commented: "How welcoming and inclusive the religion is depends on the 'fit' between your own beliefs and the ethos of your local chapel. ... I think Unitarianism struggles to embrace everyone, due to the breadth of its beliefs. This is because each Unitarian congregation is autonomous, and each has its own 'take' on Unitarian values and ethos, and range of acceptable beliefs."

### Community, compassion, and social justice

Some responses were more concerned with how Unitarians act in community. One wrote: "I know Unitarianism as the practice and spirit of a particular congregation, though this is augmented and enriched by contact with Unitarians from other congregations." Another commented: "Community is central. We come together and seek together in love." Yet another summarised their own position as follows: "To be a Unitarian is to be on a search for what you can believe, while living within an open and inclusive community of different-minded people, who are likewise embarked on their own search. Words that keep cropping up for us, which are important to us, are oneness, awareness and presence, prayer, compassion, justice and opening the mind." This emphasis on compassion and social justice was echoed by others.

**'Unitarian' no longer a relevant descriptor**
Finally, some people found the term 'Unitarian' to be "outdated and meaningless". One commented: "I have grown more sceptical over the years of the word 'Unitarian' to describe our faith, as its historical theology jars against the parallel movement of greater tolerance and other modes of religious cohesion. A part of me when asked 'What is a Unitarian?' has begun to wonder 'why do we call ourselves that?' when our movement is primarily more about the freedom of belief than it is a specific theology."

The next three questions sought to elicit the opinions of contemporary Unitarians about the key concepts of Freedom, Reason, and Tolerance.

## *Freedom of religious belief*

Freedom of religious belief is dear to the hearts of Unitarians. The alternative definitions offered for this question were fairly nuanced, as follows:

- It means that everyone has the right to work out for themselves what it is that gives their lives truth and meaning.
- It is the right to believe what your reason and conscience tell you is true.
- It is the freedom to question and doubt, and to grow into the answers. It is a process of continuous and continuing revelation.

The choices of the respondents are shown in Figure 2.2. Very few people ticked a single option; by far the most popular choice was all three combined, chosen by 156 people (61 per cent).

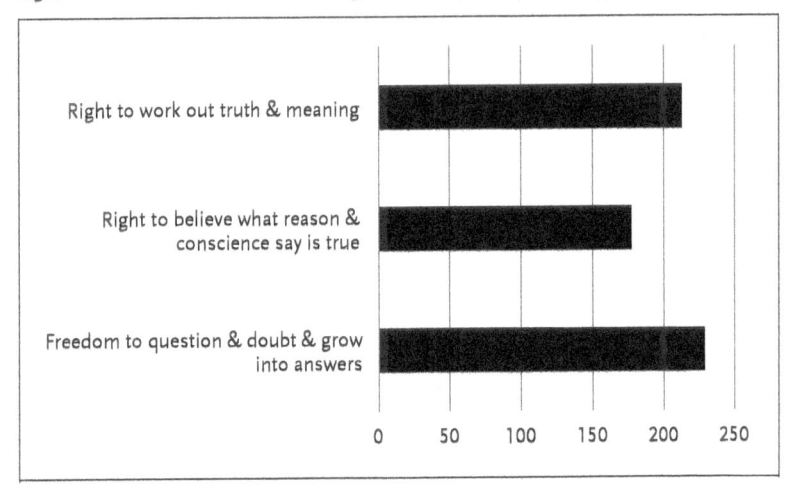

Figure 2.2: Views about Freedom of Religious Belief (from options supplied)

| Option | Count |
|---|---|
| Right to work out truth & meaning | ~210 |
| Right to believe what reason & conscience say is true | ~175 |
| Freedom to question & doubt & grow into answers | ~225 |

In spite of the popularity of the three options supplied in the questionnaire, many respondents chose to add comments. These are summarised in the shared comments below.

### Freedom of religious belief must have limits

Some participants were concerned to point out that freedom of religious belief must have some limit; thus: "We assume freedom in an environment where we grant others such freedom. In this way, our freedom remains within belief but becomes more limited in behaviour and relationship." Several expressed views similar to this: "I would make an important caveat about *acting* on belief, i.e. unless acting infringes the human rights of others." One sought to clarify the distinction between freedom of belief and freedom of activity or ritual, arguing that both were necessary: "Freedom of religious belief must also intrinsically imply freedom of religious ritual and activity, insofar as those activities do not impact on another's safety or other basic human rights." Freedom also entails responsibility, as one respondent states: "I think we need to stress it is a responsible search for truth, which takes into account 'by their fruits you will know them'." Another echoed this idea, writing: "Religious freedom is a big responsibility, because it means we must engage deeply with the questions and not answer them at an easy or superficial level."

## The open-minded sharing of ideas

Several people welcomed the personal freedom that Unitarianism gave them to be open-minded, to value diversity, and to be in a process of spiritual growth. One wrote: "It also encompasses the changes that are part of being human: we may 'grow into the answers', but the questions and the answers don't necessarily stay the same; freedom of religious belief supports this inevitably fluid situation." Respondents were clear that "community is central too…not just about personal but also about communal experience". One commented: "Ideally we do all this in a worshipping community, rather than in isolation." Another described such a community: "A market place of ideas for discussion and developing symbolic forms for contemplation and reflection".

The open-minded, open-hearted nature of Unitarian communities at their best was commented on by some. One wrote: "It is the right to participate fully in the religious community of your choice, secure in the knowledge that you are accepted for who you are." Another agreed: "It is also the freedom from discrimination or judgement, which allows equal participation in communal decision-making. When sharing in a group, it is important for individuals to feel safe and respected."

## Other views

A few respondents specifically valued the plurality of the Unitarian approach. One wrote: "It is the freedom to learn from and maybe even contribute to every branch of Christianity, other religions, and even non-religious practices. To me it means finding God wherever you look." Another was happy to be able to "belong to and follow more than one belief movement at the same time e.g. Unitarianism and Paganism". Finally, one person believed that freedom of religious belief is "a distraction, a humanist construct – it's not really possible. I am a person of faith not belief – and faith is not freely chosen, it is intimately felt. It is not a very strong opinion or a lifestyle."

## *The role of reason in Unitarian faith/spirituality*

In the past Unitarians were sometimes known as 'Rational Dissenters' because of their insistence on the use of reason in determining their religious beliefs. One participant called it "one of the basic principles of the Unitarian path in religion – the primacy of reason". This question asked contemporary Unitarians about the role of reason in their religious faith or spirituality. Respondents were invited to tick one or more of the following options:

- It helps me to work out what I believe in a responsible manner.
- If my reason and conscience accept an idea or belief, then I take it to be true.
- I am aware that sometimes reason can be fooled by our desires "so that we believe things not because they are true, but because we want to believe them"[8] (E. Burdette Backus).
- It isn't the opposite of faith; it informs my faith.
- It is the opposite of faith; it is about relying on evidence.
- It is only one part of the knowing; intuition and faith are also vital.

The choices made by the respondents are shown in Figure 2.3. The majority of respondents (199: 77 per cent) described the role of reason in their faith or spirituality by ticking a combination of options. The most popular combination was 'Work out beliefs responsibly' + 'Reason can be fooled by desires' + 'It informs my faith' + 'Only one part of the knowing' (31: 12 per

---

[8] E. Burdette Backus, quoted in Jack Mendelsohn: *Being Liberal in an Illiberal Age* (Skinner House Books, 1995, p.42).

cent). No other permutation had more than 6 per cent support. The least popular option, either alone, or in combination with others, was 'Reason is the opposite of faith'.

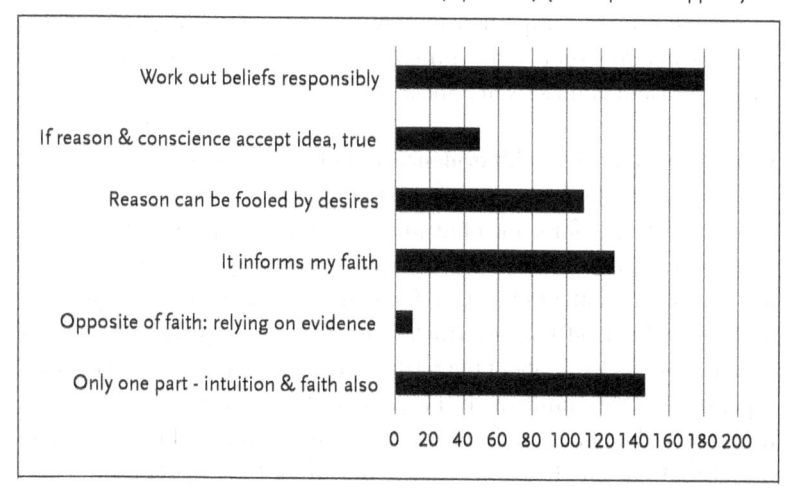

Figure 2.3: Views about the Role of Reason in Faith/Spirituality (from options supplied)

|  | |
|---|---|
| Work out beliefs responsibly | ~180 |
| If reason & conscience accept idea, true | ~45 |
| Reason can be fooled by desires | ~110 |
| It informs my faith | ~130 |
| Opposite of faith: relying on evidence | ~10 |
| Only one part - intuition & faith also | ~140 |

There was much less unanimity about this question, and consequently many comments were added. The most popular threads are summarised in the shared comments below.

## *A thinking and critical approach*

One respondent called reason "one of the core elements of Unitarianism; it is a thinking and critical approach. Its history as a reasonable faith gives the movement credibility to me and attracted me initially; I could not respect an instruction to disengage my thinking to do religion." Another concurred: "I welcome the rigour of learning what other people believe; I couldn't call myself faithful if that faith couldn't stand to be shaken." The ability to take different perspectives was welcomed by others.

### The need for spiritual engagement as well as reason
Participants were clear that reason alone does not suffice in the religious or spiritual life. One made this distinction thus: "Reason and conscience strongly influence me in rejecting certain ideas and beliefs. In accepting others, I am more cautious and leave room for possibilities which may be beyond human comprehension but seem intuitively possible." Other participants mentioned the importance of intuition and instinctive connection and faith, as well as reason.

### Reason's relationship with evidence and life experiences
One person made this comment on the idea of reason informing faith: "It's probably true for some of us in some situations. Isn't that how some scientists have made their discoveries and created progress? ... But is reason the opposite of faith? Not always. Sometimes we just have an experience that we understand but nevertheless it cannot be explained by normal reason." Others wrote about the relationship between reason and their life experiences. One commented: "I experience life through events, learning, intuition and feelings, and use my reason to interpret all this." Another found that reason "helps to make sense of and incorporate revelatory experience". A third saw it as "the ability to investigate faith and beliefs by using knowledge gained through personal and human experience".

### The limits of reason with relation to faith and spirituality
Several respondents also commented on the limits of reason in relation to faith and spirituality. One wrote: "Some days I am aware that no-one should be forced to justify their faith in things that can't be proved." Another wrote simply: "Reason would rule out miracles. My experience confirms them for me."

*Chapter 2   The meaning of 'Unitarian'; the roles of freedom, reason, and tolerance*

## *The meaning of tolerance*

The Unitarian leaflet *A Faith Worth Thinking About* presents values that Unitarians share, including "mutual respect and goodwill in personal relations" and "constructive tolerance and openness towards the sincerely held beliefs of others".[9] The next question in the survey explored Unitarian attitudes to tolerance. Participants were asked to tick one or more of the following options:

- It is an openness to new thoughts, new ideas, new people.
- It is a fierce determination to fight for the right of people to worship as they choose, so long as it doesn't harm anyone else.
- It is "loving in spite of human imperfection"[10] (Joyce Grenfell).
- It means that we can believe whatever we like, so long as it makes sense to us.
- It is accepting that others do not share our beliefs, and that their beliefs are just as valid and important to them as ours are to us.
- It is not a word I would use; I would prefer to talk about understanding and welcoming and empathy.

Participants' choices are shown in Figure 2.4. People generally ticked more than one option, with 99 (39 per cent) choosing 'Openness to the new' + 'Accepting that others do not share our beliefs' – either just those two, or in combination with other options. The rest ticked a wide variety of permutations, but only a small number opted for each combination. Further comments are summarised below.

---

9   Cliff Reed, Peter Sampson, and Matthew Smith, *A Faith Worth Thinking About: Introducing the Unitarians* (General Assembly of Unitarian & Free Christian Churches, 2010, p.4).
10  Joyce Grenfell and Katharine Moore, *An Invisible Friendship* (Futura, 1981, p.37).

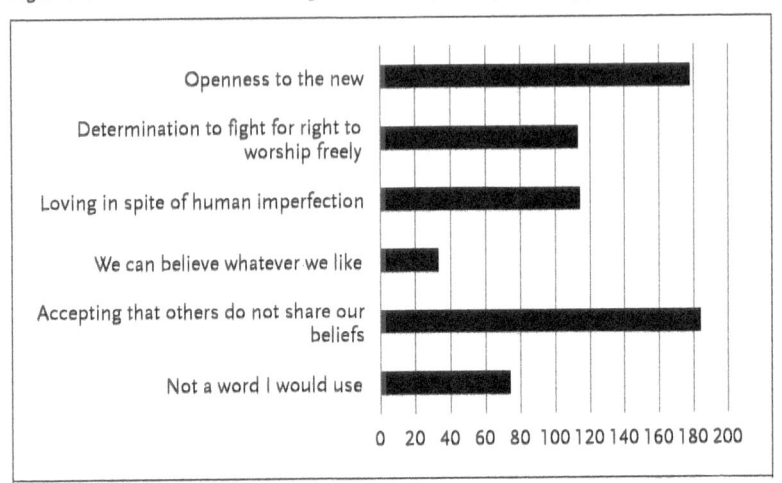

Figure 2.4: Views about the Meaning of Tolerance (from options supplied)

Tolerance, wrote one person, is "much more difficult to put into practice than to state as a precept". Other respondents developed this approach: "Tolerance is a very half-hearted, grudging type of acceptance which still seems like a vote against. But I am reduced to tolerance sometimes, as better than nothing. Then there are situations where I'd be betraying myself and many others if I didn't resist strongly, and make my views very clear and obvious."

Several emphasised that tolerance must have limits. Some argued that "personal red-line judgements about behaviour" needed to be drawn at some point, beyond which they would not tolerate the actions and ideas of others. One wrote: "The caveat is that we don't tolerate intolerance in others"; another added: "as long as it does not harm or instigate harm to others". A third stressed: "It is important to note that tolerance, like freedom, contains its own check, in that we can provide a tolerant space so long as we feel tolerated ourselves."

## Positive aspects of tolerance

Some were more constructive about the concept. One wrote: "I love the toleration bit, it means we cut people slack even when we think their beliefs aren't right." Another echoed this, commenting: "Knowing that we cannot change others, but acknowledging that others need their beliefs". More positive interpretations of tolerance included the following: "Engaging with 'the other' in a spirit of kindness"; and "Listening without thinking of arguing, leading to understanding of different subjects". One respondent believed that it meant "Accepting that others/ ourselves are at different stages of spirituality".

## Tensions and challenges of tolerance

One respondent commented: "Wilbur[11] refers to 'generous tolerance', tolerance which is not cheap and not easy, but which is costly and difficult." Another commented: "I like the word religious 'tolerance' because of the implied tension and challenge in it; it is sometimes difficult to be tolerant, but it's important and in extreme conditions prevents loss of life." One person introduced a word of caution: "We should inform ourselves so that we can question, and if necessary oppose, religious teachings/ beliefs that cause harm to followers or others. People may be free to follow their beliefs, but do we have to let what is damaging pass unchallenged?"

## Issues with the word 'tolerance', and suggestions for alternatives

Several participants took issue with the word 'tolerance' itself. More than one suggested that it implied "'putting up with' rather than an active engagement with those who are different from us". Some found the word "patronising" or "judgemental" or implying "superiority". One person was more condemnatory, commenting: "I don't like the word 'tolerance'; to me it's wishy-washy, liberals can use it to accept things that really shouldn't be accepted, like FGM [female genital mutilation]."

A number of people pondered what a better word might be. 'Acceptance' and 'respect' were proposed as possible alternatives. One argument for the

---

[11] Earl Morse Wilbur (1866–1956), American Unitarian minister, author of *Our Unitarian Heritage*.

alternatives was that "the word tolerance ... has no notion of understanding and allowing that no one faith has all the answers". Another argued: "'Tolerance' suggests that the thing you are tolerating is bad, wrong or different; 'welcoming' seems more appropriate."

## *Summary of findings*

The question was "What does the word 'Unitarian' mean to you?" It is clear that there are numerous understandings of the word. More than 75 per cent of the respondents regard it as a free religious faith, without a creed, or as an open, inclusive spiritual community; another 60 per cent believe that Unitarianism is a movement "held together by shared values and a shared approach"[12] to religion and spirituality; and 40 per cent think that Unitarianism is a Free Christian denomination, centred around the teachings of Jesus. The emphasis placed on each of these elements differs widely. Other concepts singled out as being important in attempting to define the word include those of "one-ness" or "unity"; that the Unitarian approach to religion and spirituality is a questioning and inquiring one, using reason to critically appraise beliefs; that Unitarians are inclusive and open-minded, valuing diversity; and that Unitarian communities value compassion and social justice.

All three statements offered for the question about freedom of religious belief were popular with, and important for, respondents. Through the individual comments it becomes clear that there is general agreement with the principle that freedom of religious belief must have limits, that it entails responsibility, and it requires a critical approach. Naturally the individual must decide where to set limits.

The use of reason as a tool for discerning matters of religious faith and spirituality has long been recognised in the Unitarian movement. Respondents agree that a critical and reasoned approach to matters of

---

[12] Cliff Reed, *Unitarian? What's That?: Questions and Answers about a Liberal Religious Alternative* (Lindsey Press, 1999, latest edition 2018, p.50).

religion and spirituality is important, but many accept that there is also a need for spiritual engagement, and they believe that reason alone has its limitations.

Tolerance is related in the minds of many respondents to the issue of freedom of religious belief. It is recognised that it is often difficult to put into practice. Many respondents find value in a tolerant approach to the beliefs of others, but it is clear that it must have limits, specifically that Unitarians should not tolerate particular beliefs and behaviours which are harmful to others. Some dislike the word 'tolerance' itself, suggesting that it has negative connotations. Tolerance is generally recognised as an important concept for Unitarians, but the extent of its adoption will vary from person to person and situation to situation.

## *Questions for reflection and group discussion*

1. What does the word 'Unitarian' mean to you?

2. Should there be limits to freedom of religious belief? Where would you draw the line?

3. How important is the role of reason in your own religious spiritual life?

# Chapter 3
# Religious authority; Unitarian ritual and liturgy

*Praise for minds to probe the heavens,*
*Praise for strength to breathe the air,*
*Praise for all that beauty leavens,*
*Praise for silence, music, prayer.*

Thomas H. Troeger, *Sing Your Faith*, 136

This chapter covers the second part of the section of the survey entitled 'Beliefs about Unitarianism'. Respondents were asked the following questions:

- What/who is your religious authority?
- How do you feel about the use of ritual and liturgy in worship?
- Which Unitarian rituals have you experienced/witnessed?
- How have you found the experience of this /these ritual(s)?

## Unitarians and the concept of religious authority

The question "What/who is your religious authority?" was included in order to better understand the religious and spiritual foundations of Unitarians, upon which their beliefs and actions rest. It was recognised that these might be internal or external, as Unitarians in the past hundred years or so have moved from reliance on the authority of scripture to more wide-ranging foundations, following the publication of *The Seat of Authority in*

*Religion* by James Martineau[13] in 1890. The following options were offered to respondents:

- My reason and conscience
- My lived experiences
- That of God in me – the Spirit
- Spiritual/religious teachers whose words and examples have shaped my journey
- The Bible and/or other sacred text
- Ministers/other prominent Unitarians
- My congregation.

The options chosen by respondents are shown in Figure 3.1. Once again, most people chose to tick a combination of options, the most popular of which were:

- 'Reason & conscience' + 'Lived experiences' + 'That of God in me' + 'Spiritual/ religious teachers' (29 per cent)
- 'Reason & conscience' + 'Lived experiences' (26 per cent)

The other participants ticked a variety of other options, but only a small number chose each combination. Comments made by participants fell broadly into the categories summarised below.

---

13  James Martineau (1805–1900), influential Unitarian minister, philosopher, and writer.

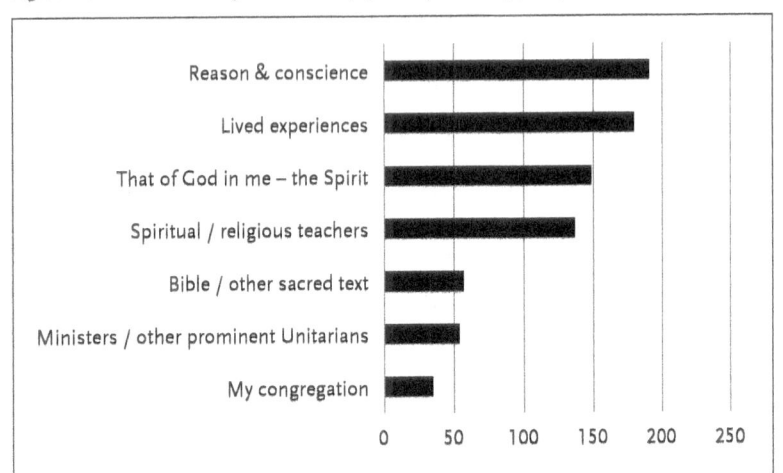

Figure 3.1: Sources of Religious Authority (from options supplied)

| Source | Value |
|---|---|
| Reason & conscience | ~195 |
| Lived experiences | ~180 |
| That of God in me – the Spirit | ~150 |
| Spiritual / religious teachers | ~140 |
| Bible / other sacred text | ~55 |
| Ministers / other prominent Unitarians | ~55 |
| My congregation | ~30 |

## Issues with the word 'authority'

Several people took issue with the word 'authority'. One wrote: "For me, 'religious authority' is a dubious idea. The insistence of sundry religious organisations that they are invested with divine authority and have all the crucial answers causes an awful lot of unnecessary strife in the world." Another commented: "I don't think I call it authority, as authority gives absolute power."

## Influence of other disciplines

Others named other disciplines as important influences on their religious and spiritual journey, such as philosophy, including rational philosophy and existentialism; social sciences, including psychology; science; literature; poetry; art; history; spirituality; travel; and meditation.

## The role of experience

Another group leaned towards the experiential, and the importance of listening to the views of others. One wrote: "My 'lived experiences' would necessarily include the general sense and explicit advice I get from a range of different people around me." Another mentioned the importance of "religious experience or being touched by the divine ... when we are open and spiritually aware, the universe provides guidance and support."

### The nature of divine authority
The importance of the Divine (whatever that might mean to the individual) as an authority was mentioned. One wrote: "Authority lies in my attempts to be at one with the universal conscience. The mind of God, if you like." Two others mentioned the teachings of Jesus as a source of authority.

### Other sources of authority
Other sources of authority cited by respondents included deep relationships with other people, the natural world, and "the presence of the universe and that it has given rise to my existence". Two mentioned the primacy of loving one's neighbour.

## *The use of ritual and liturgy in worship*

The format and content of Unitarian worship vary widely; this question was included to discover how Unitarians felt about the use of ritual and liturgy in their worship services. The four options offered were these:

- Uneasy, I prefer a worship service with little or no ritual or liturgy.
- I like the chalice lighting, because it's ours, but that's all.
- I like to worship with all my senses, and I welcome ritual and liturgy.
- I love ritual and liturgy which involves colour and sound and movement, and the chance to participate in worship.

Participants' choices are shown in Figure 3.2. Quite a large number of people ticked only one option. Sixty (23 per cent) chose 'Uneasy – prefer little or no ritual/ liturgy'; or 'Only chalice lighting'; a further 19 (7 per cent) chose both. Eighty-two (32 per cent) chose only 'Like to worship with all my senses'; or 'Love the chance to participate'. And 39 (15 per cent) chose both.

The other 57 respondents chose a different combination, or only made a comment (4: 18 per cent).

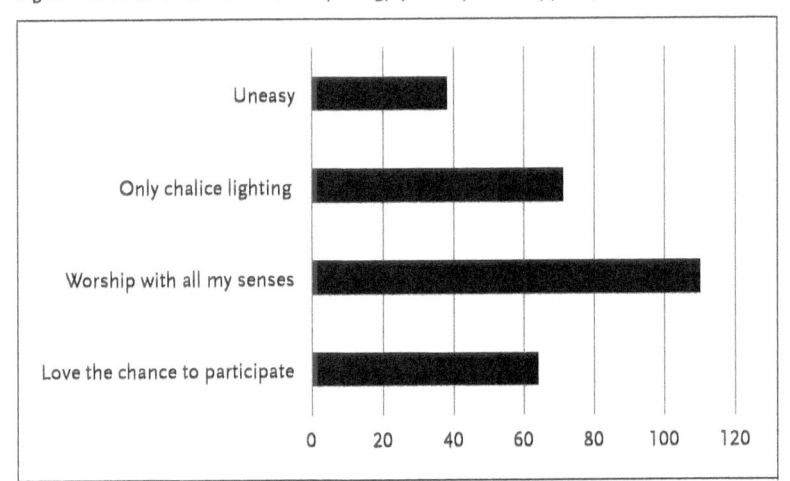

Figure 3.2: Views on the use of ritual / liturgy (from options supplied)

| Option | Value |
|---|---|
| Uneasy | ~40 |
| Only chalice lighting | ~70 |
| Worship with all my senses | ~110 |
| Love the chance to participate | ~65 |

From this it may be deduced that the participants are roughly divided into two camps: those who prefer little or no ritual or liturgy (except perhaps the chalice lighting), and those who enjoy ritual and liturgy. The comments bore this out, and are summarised below.

### Uncomfortable with ritual/liturgy

Two of the four people who commented that they disliked ritual and liturgy or were uneasy about it stated this fact without qualification. Another commented that they "prefer a simplicity in spiritual expression", and the fourth wrote of "a head vs heart debate. Love watching ritual, but head gets in the way of participation."

Others, while not being keen on ritual generally, shared experiences of being "taken out of the comfort zone" and deriving benefit from engaging with rituals in which they would not usually have participated; one wrote: "I experienced a small group communion a few years ago at GA [which] moved me greatly – it was wonderful!". Another commented: "I have benefited from activities that are not naturally 'me' e.g. walking a labyrinth." However, another person described being made to feel "very uncomfortable on occasions, where I have visited services where you are given no choice (or prior warning) but to participate i.e. drawing and presenting/ explaining your efforts, or being asked to speak, turning round & shaking hands, etc."

### Lukewarm or indifferent towards ritual/liturgy

Several participants were lukewarm about the use of ritual and liturgy in services, or else were indifferent towards them. One wrote: "I could do without ritual, but many newcomers seem to find it rewarding, and enjoy participating. So I don't mind, but sometimes it's distracting to me." A similar but contrasting view was shared by another person, who commented: "I'm lukewarm. I fear it deters outsiders. But I can't see an alternative." Another warned against too much ritual or liturgy in a service, commenting: "Generally, chalice lighting plus a responsive reading is ample. Overdoing things can drown the 'still small voice'." And one respondent genuinely had no preference, writing: "To me worship can be done just as easily alone as with others, at home, outdoors, or in chapel, with ritual or with nothing at all. There is a place for all of it. The ritual provides a framework and it can be comforting ... just as long as it doesn't hinder things."

### Enjoyment of ritual/liturgy

Respondents who liked ritual and liturgy did so for three reasons. First, they were seen as providing some structure and familiarity to a service. One person commented: "I appreciate the value of ritual – the bonding that comes with hymn singing." A worship leader stated that "a familiar form (whether ritual or liturgy or both) used regularly is a comfort for a congregation"; and "those who come from a background where liturgy was used seem to welcome that in a Unitarian service". The second reason for liking ritual and liturgy was that it "creates a sense of community, common purpose". One respondent added that "simply agreeing to meet together to participate in worship is a 'ritual'." The third reason was that ritual can introduce a non-verbal element into the service; one wrote: "I think some ritual (colour, sound, movement) has value/ mystery." Another suggested that it may have "a role in establishing a feeling of a 'sacred place'".

Several respondents were enthusiastic about participatory or experimental services; one explained: "I support forms of ritual, music, and a form of liturgy which involves colour and sound and movement, and the chance to participate in worship that explores aspects of beliefs from a variety of directions." Particular elements of the service were singled out for praise; one person valued "the peace and tranquillity of a service", and another wrote: "I would include periods of shared silence as one of the most popular [rituals] we have." Music or singing was a key part of the service for some people.

### Quality and relevance are key to good ritual/liturgy
Some respondents argued that the quality and relevance of any ritual and liturgy were "the key indicators of good worship". This was seen as dependent on the worship leader. One wrote: "I like ritual in worship so long as it is carried out in a manner that is 'seemly and reverent' (to borrow an Anglican phrase). I don't like ritual that seems hastily thrown together."

### The distinction between ritual and liturgy
A few participants drew a distinction between ritual and liturgy. One wrote: "I enjoy and feel moved by ritual, but am ambivalent towards liturgy." Another commented: "I like liturgy and some ritual – but it does depend, surely, on whether a particular liturgy speaks to me?" Conversely, one wrote: "Not too comfortable with words that are unchanging from service to service" – an issue with set liturgy, which is less common in Unitarian worship these days than in the past.

### All worship contains ritual and liturgy
However, two people pointed out firmly that "All worship in groups has ritual and liturgy, even if the ritual is so informal that it is hard to identify it" and that "Liturgy is everything we do in worship: it is the 'work of the people'".

Finally, some respondents regretted that there was not more ritual and liturgy in Unitarian worship services. One wrote: "Services that rely purely on talking make me feel a bit ... bored and disconnected." Another commented: "You could call me a 'high' 'catholic?!' Unitarian – as I sometimes use icons, rote prayers, prayer beads in my personal spiritual practice – even though I don't push this on my congregation when leading worship."

## *Experience of Unitarian rituals*

Following on from the last question, respondents were asked which Unitarian rituals they had experienced or witnessed. The seven most common rituals were offered as options:

- Lighting the Chalice
- Candles of Joy and Concern
- Communion
- Flower Communion
- The Lord's Prayer (sung)
- The Lord's Prayer (said)
- Other words in which the whole congregation join, for example, a covenant.

Figure 3.3 shows the rituals that respondents have experienced (from the options supplied).

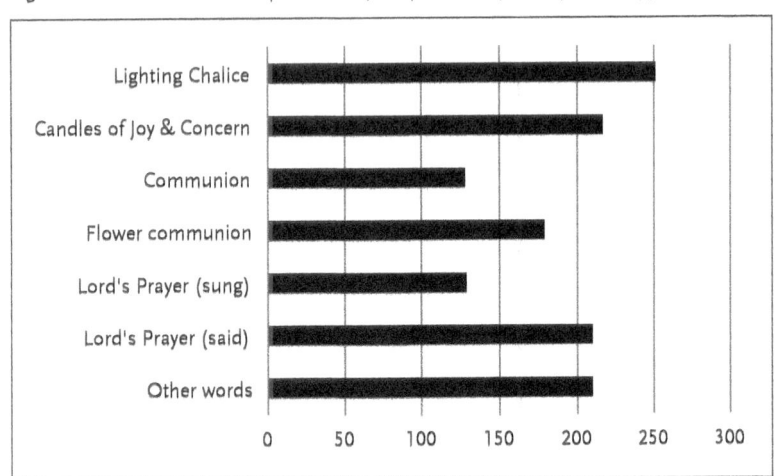

Figure 3.3: Unitarian Rituals experienced by Respondents (from options supplied)

| Ritual | Count |
|---|---|
| Lighting Chalice | ~255 |
| Candles of Joy & Concern | ~215 |
| Communion | ~130 |
| Flower communion | ~180 |
| Lord's Prayer (sung) | ~130 |
| Lord's Prayer (said) | ~210 |
| Other words | ~210 |

Fifty-nine (23 per cent) ticked all seven options. Respondents used the 'Other' box to list the very many other rituals that they had witnessed or experienced. These included the following:

- Sung introits, benedictions
- Responsive prayers/readings
- Water communion/gathering the waters
- Rituals involving objects e.g. stones, feathers, flowers, prayer beads, wool, cord
- Various kinds of communion – chocolate, fruit, etc.
- Fellowship or community ritual/the Peace
- Sharing bread (not communion) or meals
- Rites of passage
- Symbolic candle lighting (not Candles of Joy & Concern)/ passing round a lighted chalice
- Maze/Labyrinth walk
- Solstice celebrations
- Pagan/Earth Spirit rituals

*Chapter 3   Religious authority; Unitarian ritual and liturgy*

- Dancing
- Sharing affirmations/posting on a prayer tree
- Membership/commitment ritual
- One-off rituals for particular occasions
- Silent, meditative walking
- Procession in at the start, out at the end.

This list is unlikely to be representative of the Unitarian community as a whole, but it does show the wide variety of rituals practised in Unitarian communities.

As a supplementary question, respondents were asked to describe their own experience of these rituals in Unitarian worship services. The responses are summarised in Figure 3.4 , and in the shared comments.

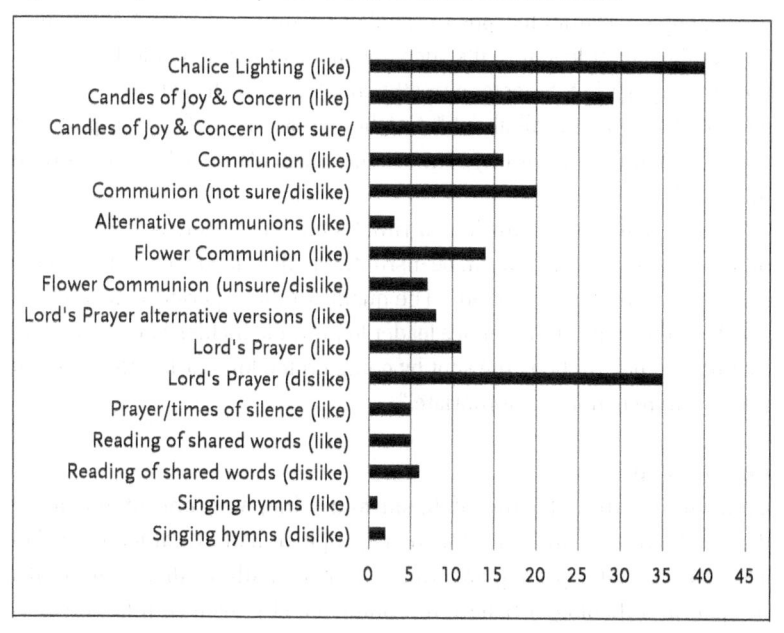

Figure 3.4: Respondents' Responses to some common Unitarian Rituals

### Chalice Lighting

The Chalice Lighting was the one Unitarian ritual mentioned in the options about which there were no negative or even ambivalent comments. Some saw it as "an essential aspect of every service: a very meaningful, symbolic act". It was valued as "a visible and uplifting boundary to our special time together" by some, and for "the connection it (and associated chalice readings) gives me with other Unitarians". One person commented: "Chalice lighting is an essential ritual in terms of making our services feel 'religious' ... and also in terms of reminding the congregation of our connection to something bigger."

Other Unitarian rituals attracted both positive and negative views. One respondent commented wryly: "I've loved and loathed most of them at different times."

### Candles of Joy and Concern

Most people commented positively about Candles of Joy and Concern. One enthused: "I love it ... it's such a wonderful way to get to know your fellow congregation, to foster empathy, and for me really gets to the crux of what Unitarianism is all about." Another wrote: "It is of vital importance in strengthening community connections ... articulating what is important to us all."

Others had issues with it as a ritual. One wrote: "great to hear what others wish to present, but can be disruptive to the mood and rhythm of the service". Another commented: "The quality of the experience depends so much on the skills of the service leader to promote inclusiveness – ensure that no one person hogs the spot by going on too long or by talking about issues that may not be appropriate."

### Communion

Communion (the sharing of bread and wine) was one of the more divisive Unitarian rituals as, for many people, it had unwanted Christian associations. One participant found it "personally challenging, as it's not part of a theology I believe in". Someone else disliked it because "as practised by Unitarians [it] is too often a pale imitation of orthodox practice which I personally find embarrassing and distasteful". Because of such perceptions, it is generally offered as an optional and occasional ritual after the regular Sunday service.

Some respondents enjoyed it "as a celebration of our spiritual community". One commented: "Communion at our chapel engenders a feeling of togetherness." Another called it "a sublime spiritual experience". Alternative communion services (featuring chocolate or fruit, for example) were liked by those who commented on them. The Flower Communion received mixed reviews; one enthusiast wrote: "I particularly like the Flower Communion as an alternative, particularly because of the way Norbert Capek[14] used it to further inclusiveness." However, some people were ambivalent about it, describing it as "inadequate", "slightly embarrassing", and even "trivial and precious"

**The Lord's Prayer**
The most contentious example of liturgy for the respondents was undoubtedly the recitation of the Lord's Prayer. It had some support, but more detractors (see Figure 3.4 above). One supporter wrote: "I find saying the Lord's Prayer meaningful even if I don't literally believe the traditional form of words ... it transcends the individual, yet in spirit remains personal. I find the rhythm and familiarity of the traditional version calming." Another commented: "To learn the Lord's Prayer at a young age is a ritual, but its meaning, as life progresses, is a profound experience."

Some simply no longer related to the Lord's Prayer, and would not say or sing it, while respecting that it still had meaning for others. Others objected to its content, such as the person who wrote: "I don't like the assumption that we need to pray to a 'God', that the 'God' is masculine, that he lives in heaven, that he is the power and the glory, and I don't like the way it asks for things." Another, disliking the sung Lord's Prayer, wrote: "Thankfully ... (it) ... is on the decline – two or three well-known settings – dreadful, cloying Victoriana." Some of the participants who disliked the traditional form of the Lord's Prayer *did* like alternative, contemporary versions. One wrote:

---

14  Norbert Capek (1870–1942), the founder of the modern Unitarian church in the Czech Republic.

"I am very happy with alternative words that provide the same meaning." Another commented: "The Unitarian versions of it I've experienced have worked well for me."

Other prayers and times of silence were appreciated by those who commented on them. One wrote: "A period of communal silence is probably the best ritual, if well facilitated." Another commented: "Some reflective music to follow a silence extends the space, while gently bringing one back to the here and now of the service."

### The sharing of words
Respondents who liked sharing words together appreciated the feeling of inclusivity and togetherness that this created; however, one person wrote: "I prefer not to say words in which the whole congregation joins, it feels a little too like the Creed. This is an emotional response ... reason allows me to see that the words spoken are open, inclusive, and often beautiful."

### General comments about ritual and liturgy
Many found both ritual and liturgy to be positive and meaningful. One participant wrote: "These experiences are very stimulating, they break the routine, and I feel more connected with the divine and others in the congregation." Another commented: "I find that liturgy and symbolic actions can add extra dimensions that aren't present in gatherings where only words are used." Another group commented on the way in which rituals brought them into community with their fellow worshippers. One wrote: "I think that all these rituals give the congregation an opportunity to be an active part of worship, and a chance to feel a sense of belonging to a community." Others wrote of the internal effects that participating in Unitarian rituals had on them; words such as "calming", "elevating", "quietening", "challenging", "peaceful", "comforting" and "reassuring" were used. One commented: "They help to bring me more deeply into worship."

### The importance of variety
The importance of having variety in Unitarian rituals was remarked on by some. One wrote: "I enjoy having a variety of ritual, and on occasion none

at all." Another commented: "I enjoy diversity and variety, and using words, songs, prayers from other faiths and beliefs." This was underscored by those who commented on their dislike of repetition in rituals. One wrote: "Repetitive use of the same bit of ritual, for example to end a service, I find very irritating, as if I am being trapped." Another commented: "Ritual can enhance worship, but if it becomes stale it can have the opposite effect."

### The importance of the worship leader
Some commented on the vital role of the worship leader in the delivery of meaningful ritual. One wrote: "It's more about the intent of the person conducting the ritual, the energy they bring, how the rest of the people are engaged, what does it leave with me in my heart?" Another wrote of the importance of worship being "offered and shared in reverence". A third warned: "The use of ritual needs to be carefully planned, and if possible rehearsed; badly done ritual can be very messy and become embarrassing and distract from a sense of spiritual uplift."

## *Summary of findings*

The responses to the question "What/who is your religious authority?" were very significant. The question was included in the survey in order to better understand the religious and spiritual foundations of Unitarians, upon which their beliefs and actions rest. Nearly three-quarters of the participants chose "My reason and conscience" and/or "My lived experiences"; and 58 per cent chose "That of God in me – the Spirit". In other words, the most popular choices were those which did not rely on the opinions and judgement of others. Many respondents wrote of "influences" rather than "sources of authority", with 53 per cent mentioning "spiritual/religious teachers", while sacred texts such as the Bible, or ministers and other prominent Unitarians, attracted around 20 per cent each. This indicates that the spiritual lives of the respondents are built on a variety of foundations, but that a majority rely on their own consciences, lived experiences, and promptings from the Spirit.

The use of ritual and liturgy in worship divided participants into two camps: those who are uneasy about them and prefer a minimal use of them, and those who enjoy and welcome them as part of the worship service. The uneasiness is grounded mainly in a reluctance to participate in group activities during a worship service. Those who like them do so for a variety of reasons: that they provide some structure and familiarity to a service; that they create a sense of community in the congregation; and that ritual introduces a non-verbal element into worship. Quality and relevance are seen as key factors: relevant and well-delivered ritual can be uplifting – and ill-prepared ritual quite the opposite.

It is clear that the views of the respondents on the use of ritual and liturgy in worship are many and varied: some are indifferent, some are wary, some like them, some love them, and some dislike them. There seems to be little correlation between age and gender on this issue: respondents of all ages and genders have varied viewpoints. The only ritual to be universally appreciated is the chalice lighting; all the others have both supporters and detractors.

To sum up, the attitude of Unitarians towards ritual in worship services may best be described as 'mixed'. Some love it, and think there is not enough; some do not mind it, so long as it is relevant and meaningful to them; and some are not keen on it at all. Respondents' comments suggest a feeling that it is becoming more welcomed and acceptable as time goes by and worship patterns and structures change and develop.

## *Questions for reflection and group discussion*

1. On what do you base your religious/spiritual beliefs or position?

2. How much ritual and/or liturgy do you like in a Unitarian worship service?

3. Which Unitarian rituals are most meaningful to you?

# Chapter 4
# *Unitarian views on morality; sexuality, gender, and marriage; inclusion and equality*

> *You must be true unto yourself*
> *If truth to others you would teach;*
> *Your soul must overflow with love*
> *If you another's soul would reach.*
>
> After Horatius Bonar, *Hymns for Living*, 155

The third section of the survey addressed questions concerning Unitarian morality and values. The next two chapters will deal with respondents' answers to these. This chapter will discuss the questions concerned with the way Unitarians live in the world, and their attitudes to how others live in it.

- What does morality mean to you as a Unitarian?
- What are your views on gender, sexuality, and marriage?
- What are your views on inclusion and equality?

## Unitarian views on morality

In order to prompt reflection on this issue, respondents were offered five options:

- It is about being open and inclusive and welcoming, to all people, all ideas.

- It must be a system of thought and belief which can be lived by, not just pretty words.
- It is about compassion: it must lead us to being kinder, more loving, to ourselves, other people, and the world.
- It is about respecting the beliefs and life journeys of others; we are all on a spiritual journey towards God/the Divine/unitive consciousness.
- It is about living out the Unitarian values of freedom of belief, based on reason and conscience, accepting the right of others to do the same.

Participants were invited to tick all the options that applied. The results are shown in Figure 4.1. Many participants chose more than one of the options given; indeed, the most popular combination was all five options, chosen by 61 (24 per cent). Others chose a wide variety of permutations. The answers to the question "What does morality mean to you?" were varied and complex. The main threads are summarised in the shared comments below.

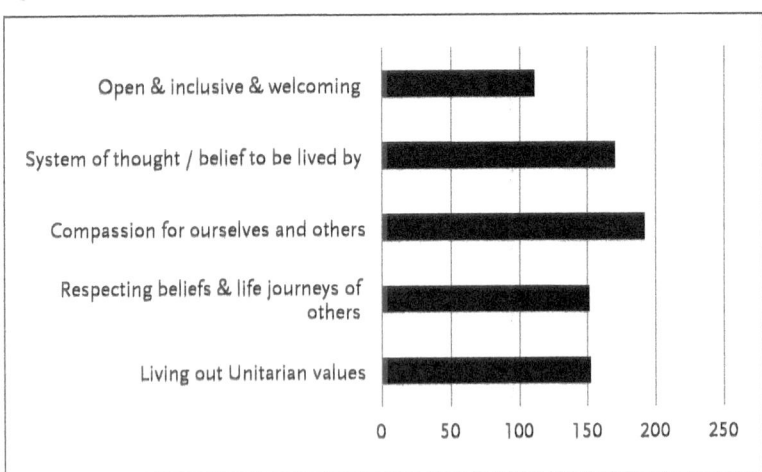

Figure 4.1: Views on Morality (from options supplied)

## Defining the term 'morality'

A few respondents wanted to clarify the term 'morality' itself. One wrote: "Morality is a top–down imposition of a moral code, e.g. the Ten Commandments. I live by ethics which emerge from our embodiment and situatedness in the physical world." Another commented:

> Morality is a sub-set of ethics. I believe ethics to be the range of all possible ordered responses to what is going on around us. Morality for me is that subset of possible responses that struggles to balance the needs of the whole human family, and increasingly the needs of other organisms, against the needs of the individual human (or animal) who has suffered a particular life path. Not always do the needs of the many overwhelm the needs of the one (or smaller group). Morality entails self-discipline, struggle, and humility.

## External expectations are also important

One person warned that morality "has to take account of societal, cultural, and family expectations, unfortunately". Another enlarged on this, writing:

> Morality or ethics may be understood, after Foucault, as the relation that one has with oneself that is manifested as the 'considered practice of freedom', and that is constituted in the self in its relation to others. Consequently, moral and ethical questions have to be considered in the context of social, political, and economic power relations, as such powers may either suppress or encourage this considered practice of freedom, and have strategies that frame the acquisition of ethics and morality themselves. The Unitarian tradition, as I see it, is one that has sought to encourage the considered practice of freedom – not for oneself at the expense of others, but for all.

## Morality is about doing, not believing

As we saw in Figure 4.1, many respondents were clear that morality must be a system of thought and belief by which people live, not just words. Some wished to extend this. One wrote: "It must be a system of thought and belief which we aim to live by, strive towards, reflect on, and improve." Another commented: "It's about living out my Unitarian values of love, welcoming difference, living authentically for the goodness of humanity."

For others, it meant "one's sense of right and wrong and one's choice for right". One wrote: "It's about doing what's right, according to human decency and kindness, even if it's hard or has negative consequences for us." Another commented: "Morality means bringing all of our faculties (rational, emotional, spiritual) to discerning right and wrong (forming and influencing our conscience) and then acting on that as best we can."

### Is morality about respecting the beliefs of others?

Some took issue with the idea that Unitarians should automatically respect others' beliefs; one wrote: "If a person believes I should be executed for being gay ... then I don't respect that or them. If a person believes in the literal truth of the Bible or any sacred book, then I don't respect that either, because ... it often leads to hatred. I appreciate this reveals a hierarchy of beliefs and values, but I'm entirely comfortable with that. Some beliefs are not worth respecting." Another commented dryly: "While it's nice to be fluffy about accepting other beliefs, we don't really have much time for it ... if we were to be asked to have a 'sacred heart of Jesus' figurine at the front of the church, we wouldn't be impressed."

The above comments perhaps highlight some discrepancies in Unitarian attitudes towards tolerance of the beliefs of others, as discussed in Chapter 2. It seems that in their own worship and practice, there may be significant areas of intolerance or non-acceptance. The wide Unitarian embrace of the beliefs of others does not necessarily mean that "anything goes". What may be acceptable in some congregations will not be so in others, and some beliefs and practices (rightly) will not be acceptable in any congregation.

### Morality as a spiritual challenge

Some participants saw morality as a challenge; one wrote about "being progressive and maybe a bit weird for your own times, but perhaps perceived as a revolutionary". Another appreciated "how the challenge of being a congregation member, and of the call to witness to the community and world, holds me up to a higher moral standard". A third commented that "it requires us to be able to disagree with others and stand up for what is right, even if that is the unpopular stance". Some wrote of "spiritual integrity"; of "being strong and able to be true to myself"; and of "finding an authentic religious life for ourselves".

**Some guiding principles concerning morality**
A few respondents listed the guiding principles that they believed morality should include: love, faith, truth, peace, non-violence in thought, word, and deed, having respect for each other, and honesty. One regretted the fact that "The problem with being creedless is that we avoid having a set of ethical statements" and asked: "Have past GA decisions on ethical matters ever been gathered together in some accessible form?"[15]

Compassion was an option ticked by nearly three-quarters of all participants. Several also felt moved to comment further on it. One wrote: "It must centre on compassion for others, including our non-human planet-mates." And another wrote: "It should be about acting out our beliefs, and living our morality with care and compassion; viewing life through how those who experience disadvantage might perceive it."

**A liberal approach to faith?**
Some respondents commented positively on the Unitarian "liberal approach to faith", but others took issue with the first option: that of being open and inclusive and welcoming, to all people, all ideas. One wrote: "I was going to tick box 1, but inclusive of or welcoming ALL ideas? Do we need to qualify that to say 'ideas that do no [intentional] harm'?" Another echoed this, commenting: "Even as a Unitarian, however inclusive I try to be, I still think there need to be perimeters of morality – outside which I will try not to stray – even though I accept that the perimeters may be

---

[15] To which the answer is yes: it is possible to obtain a list of past successful resolutions from Unitarian Headquarters at Essex Hall, and the national website includes a section called "What we stand for" (https://www.unitarian.org.uk/pages/what-we-stand, accessed 27 October 2017).

wider/ narrower for others. It's not a case of anything goes – I can't accept and welcome all ideas/ behaviours." Another was troubled by

> the tendency I sometimes see for Unitarians to use liberalism almost as an excuse not to challenge views and acts which are harmful to others (or to act as if liberalism means being agnostic about questions of right and wrong altogether and therefore refusing to judge about good and evil ... personally I think this sort of abstention is immoral in itself). Of course many moral questions are extremely complex and hard to resolve, but I think we are called to engage with them anyway. There are definitely ideas I do not feel obliged to be inclusive and welcoming of ... and I wonder if a stronger statement of our shared values and principles would make that clearer in our communities.

## *Gender, sexuality, and marriage*

Unitarian views on gender, sexuality, and marriage are complex and wide-ranging. Respondents were offered five options, one of which, Option 4, confusingly conflated the concepts of same-sex or equal marriage with polyamorous marriage, which some respondents either picked up on, or struggled with. If the two had been separated, the number of people in favour of same-sex/ equal marriage would undoubtedly have been higher. The five options were as follows:

- A person's sexuality or gender should not bar them from fulfilling any role in their lives, whether private or public.
- A person's sexuality is nobody's business but their own, so long as it is consensual.
- Marriage should be between a man and a woman.
- Marriage can be between two or more people of whatever gender.
- Everyone, of whatever sexual orientation, should make a principled effort to understand how people of different sexual orientations feel and think, as individuals.

The options chosen by respondents are shown in Figure 4.2. The only single option to attract many respondents was the first: that sexuality or gender should not bar a person from fulfilling any role in their lives, with 14 people (5 per cent) choosing this option only. Popular combinations of options combined this with other options, the most common being all options except 'Marriage between a man and a woman' (73: 28 per cent) and 'No bar' + 'Nobody's business' + 'Try to understand' (46: 18 per cent). The other respondents chose a wide variety of combinations, but only a small number opted for each combination. As may be expected, this question attracted a wide variety of comments, which are summarised below.

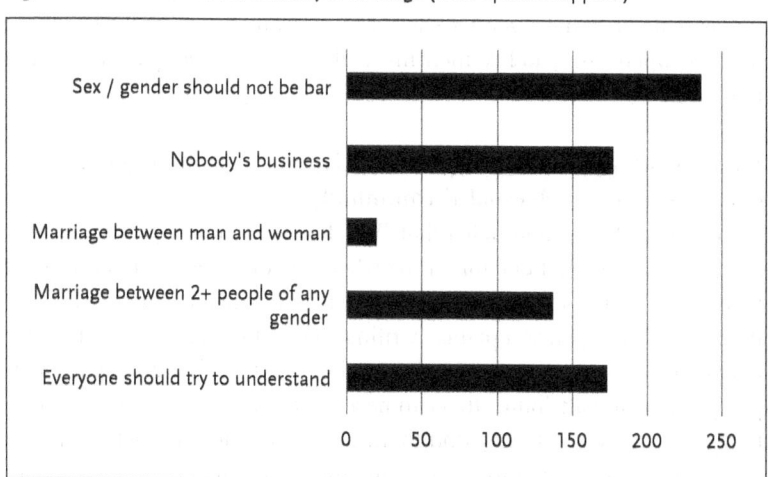

Figure 4.2: Views on Gender, Sexuality & Marriage (from options supplied)

One person summed up the complexity very neatly: "What a huge and complex question. So much of what is acceptable in relation to gender, sexuality, marriage is determined by culture, economics, the political climate. Then religion is invoked to back up the majority opinion, based on what most people feel is the safe thing to do. So I am nervous about giving definitive answers here, except to say that all human relationships must be based on appreciating the worth and dignity of each other and an absence of exploitation of any kind." Two others echoed this, writing: "Love is love. Who am I to judge what is right for another?" and "What matters is that relationships are genuine and caring and non-abusive."

## Celebrating diversity

Several participants believed that all varieties of sexual orientation and gender identity should be "celebrated as part of natural human diversity". One wrote simply: "People are people; we are all individuals, each with our own ways of being and doing things. There are things we can't help about our own character or how we are, such as height, eye colour, length of fingers, genes, skin colour, parentage and sexuality, among many other things." Another remarked: "I have always tried to see people as people and not as male or female, gender should be of no matter – everyone should have the opportunity to live their life as they see fit, as long as it does not harm anyone else."

## Views about the LGBTQIA+ (Lesbian, Gay, Bisexual, Transgender, Queer, Intersexual, Asexual +) community

Some stated clearly their belief that "We should accept people of whatever sexuality. We should hope for a time when it is unnecessary to be defined by one's sexual orientation, and accepted for our personhood." Another made a plea for open acceptance, writing: "Lots of research shows that gay people, using whatever nomenclature they see fit, often have particular perspectives and attributes that can be a positive and unique contribution to the society in which they find themselves, so society as a whole, not to mention the next generation of struggling young queers, has a stake in ensuring that LGBTQ etc people are able to be themselves in a completely open way – and vice versa."

One respondent decided against Option 2 ('A person's sexuality is nobody's business but their own, so long as it is consensual') "because this view is sometimes used as a kind of excuse by people who want to seem tolerant but who would rather LGBTQ+ people stop talking about their experiences. But if LGBTQ+ people want to keep their sexuality or gender private, of course they should be able to. I would love to see Unitarians become better informed about gender, sexuality, and relationship diversity." Another person recognised that times were changing, and struggled with their own attitude: "It's so easy to tick a box! I've ticked the ones which I genuinely think I agree with, but I must admit to being challenged when I meet with some situations in actuality."

**Sexuality issues**
Two people commented about the sexual relationship itself. One wrote: "Sex shouldn't be exclusive to people in marriages/ relationships. It is for humankind to enjoy, and there's nothing wrong with people having sex just for fun, as long as it's consensual, enjoyed responsibly, and doesn't hurt anybody." The other called sex "the driver of human existence" and suggested that it needs to be "understood in its entirety".

Despite the large majority of respondents who ticked the 'No bar' option, two people expressed concerns about the potential for gender or sexual orientation to cause particular issues. One wrote: "A person's sexuality may need to be revealed when seeking employment in certain areas where it may expose them to exploitation, e.g. certain Government jobs."

The word "consensual" in Option 2 raised concerns in the minds of some. One commented that "any sexual act has to be legal as well as consensual, e.g. not rape, paedophilia and other crimes". Another wrote that they had ticked the first box "on the basis that it was not meant to include non-consensual sexual orientations or deviancies". A third described consensuality as "a grey area, as it can be difficult to determine what 'consensual' actually means. People can be put under pressure to 'consent' or may 'consent' out of fear, and that obviously isn't right."

**Same-sex/equal marriage ... polyamorous marriage**
Although the conflation in the option may have created problems, it did generate some perceptive comments. One respondent wrote: "Marriage should be between two people of whatever gender. I don't think that polygamy is immoral or wrong – it may be the best choice in some circumstances or cultures – but I do think that it tends to promote more inequality and that this is usually to the detriment of women." Another commented: "I

have an open mind on polyamory, but I am not at present convinced that the law should provide for a consensual polyamorous relationship to be designated 'marriage'." One person spoke out in favour of polyamorous relationships: "Stable, honest, and loving polyamorous relationships are just as valid as any other relationships and should be treated as such." Others had reservations: one person did "not personally feel comfortable in extending marriage to polyamorous/ polygamous relationships/ multiple partners", while another commented: "I suppose more than two persons to a 'marriage' is feasible – but the 'legal' rights, as understood by society, would be very difficult to account for."

### Views about marriage

Several participants were keen to comment on what marriage should entail. One wrote: "Marriage should be between two people, and a serious, long-term commitment." Another commented that marriage "is also a legal contract and thus reflects social/civil consensus". A third had a different view, commenting: "I see marriage as belonging to the church and feel strongly that they should be allowed to dictate its parameters. As it is, I am shocked by how participants spend a lot of money without ever attending again."

Twenty respondents (8 per cent) ticked 'Marriage should be between a man and a woman', and some also made comments about this. One wrote: "I must respect the view of many that 'marriage' implies a relationship between a man and a woman. Nevertheless, by default of an alternative accepted terminology, I am accepting of the current 'same-sex' marriage." Another felt that "marriage is not the right word for same-sex partnerships, though I am very happy for them to exist. I feel marriage has to be between a male and a female for the procreation of children and would like there to be another word to define a same-sex union." A third commented: "I wish there was a ceremony that held all the solemnity, meaning, and commitment as the ones between M and F, but could be given a different name."

One person argued that "Marriage (as regulated in this country) is a contract in law pertaining to property and finance. I would prefer to follow the French example, where a marriage ceremony is a civil ceremony, which is then followed by a blessing in church for those who wish it." A second respondent echoed this thought.

**Issues about children**
A few respondents raised concerns about children. One believed that same-sex couples should not bring children up; another that the current age of consent "should be upheld despite its frequent violation"; and a third commented: "I do have concerns about children who are brought into this world in order to satisfy parents, straight or gay, where using surrogates involves a third-party donor rather than both parents. I fear identity issues and possible mental-health issues for the children."

Finally, one person thought that the issues of sexuality, gender identity, and same-sex marriage have "become too predominant in our movement". This view is not borne out by the majority of respondents, but all of the above comments illustrate the wide variety of views and a considerable degree of uncertainty and confusion over these issues.

## *Unitarians and inclusion and equality*

The issues of inclusion and equality are closely related to the previous question. People were offered the following options, and their choices are presented in Figure 4.3.

- They are central to my life, and the main reason why I was attracted to Unitarianism.
- Everyone is human, and is entitled to equal respect and opportunities.
- They are good ideals, but hopelessly unrealistic – the real world just doesn't work like that.
- Our congregations as well as we as individuals need to be open and inclusive and welcoming.
- There has to be a limit to how inclusive and welcoming we are, as congregations.

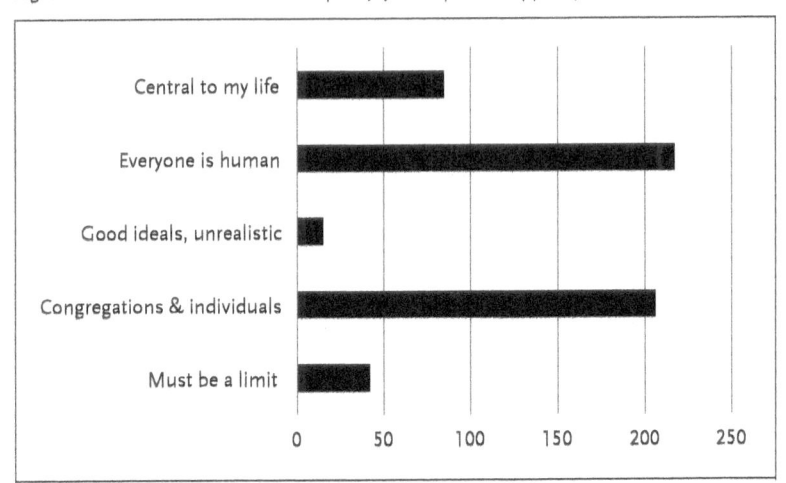

Figure 4.3: Views on Inclusion and Equality (from options supplied)

|  | |
|---|---|
| Central to my life | ~85 |
| Everyone is human | ~215 |
| Good ideals, unrealistic | ~15 |
| Congregations & individuals | ~205 |
| Must be a limit | ~40 |

Thirty-five respondents chose a single option: 'Everyone is human' (24: 9 per cent) or 'Congregations and individuals need to be inclusive and welcoming' (11: 4 per cent). Far more (88: 24 per cent) chose these two options as a combination. The other popular combination of options was 'Central to my life' + 'Everyone is human' + 'Congregations and individuals need to be inclusive and welcoming' (62: 24 per cent). The comments for this question were generally either in favour of inclusion and equality, or stated reasons why there should be some limits to them. They are summarised in the shared comments below.

### General reflections on inclusion and equality
One person commented about the meaning of the term 'inclusion': "Everyone should have equal access to opportunities. If inclusion in this context means that everyone has a right to be included within society as a whole, and no-one should be excluded from having access to opportunities that society as a whole deems reasonable, then yes, I believe in inclusion. However, this is a very broad reasoning of inclusion in the context of equality." Another believed that "inequality [is a] cause of major problems;

therefore we should strive for a more equal society, while also recognising that the differences between individuals are of value and should be respected." Several people commented that although inclusion and equality might be unrealistic ideals, as the third option posits, the attempt should nevertheless be made. One wrote: "Why not reach for the moon and stars?" Another commented: "There should always be room for more inclusivity, and we should think about it and try to achieve it, all the time; again, quite difficult to put into practice."

## Inclusion within Unitarian communities

The most frequent comments on this question were about the role of inclusion *within* Unitarian communities. Some were strongly in favour of it. One wrote: "Again, it's in the name. We're Unitarians. I know this was originally to do with the Unity of God, but that's not what it means to us now." Another affirmed: "We are all different and with different gifts, and we shouldn't be prejudiced against people different from us just because they are different." A third commented: "We should try to welcome all those who come with good intentions."

Not all responses were so positive. Some were concerned about the "fit" with the Unitarian ethos. One wrote: "Anyone wishing to join the movement whose attitudes and behaviour are out of step with the principles and values of the General Assembly Object[16] would, I feel, be likely to be uncomfortable within the movement, and the movement uncomfortable with them." One participant suggested that "churches and chapels ... have their own limits of time, energy and money, and therefore will not be a place of care and comfort for everyone". Another found "living the reality" of inclusion difficult, and commented: "For example, we sometimes have people coming into church asking for water or money, and I don't know where the line is between being inclusive and welcoming and looking after ourselves and our safety." One respondent stated bluntly: "Unitarians are NOT as inclusive as they claim; therefore they treat people differently." Another wrote: "I think we as individuals and congregations

---

16 Printed in full on page 182.

need to be aware of our limits to inclusivity and gain support/ training and understanding around it."

### Extreme beliefs or behaviours not welcomed – what are the limits?

Quite a number of participants were clear that people holding extreme beliefs harmful to others would not be welcomed in Unitarian communities. Some listed beliefs or behaviours which would not be welcomed, for example extremist, fascist, or murderous attitudes; paedophilia; racism; homophobia; and any mental, physical, or sexual cruelty. Another commented: "There also need to be procedures to exclude destructive people – and, unfortunately, destructive people do exist." Another person wrote: "There will always be limits to our inclusion i.e. can/ should we tolerate the intolerant, or those whose behaviour and views actively seek to harm and undermine our communities?"

The notion of "hate the sin but love the sinner" was raised by some respondents. One asked: "Should we distinguish between the values some people hold and the people that hold them? Do the values that you hold undermine my very being? Do they chip away at my dignity and my worth as a member of the human race? There can be no simple answer to such a complex question. It has to be one that we answer as a particular situation arises, and we deal with it fortified by our tradition, our faith, our humanity, our hope."

The inclusion of people with mental-health problems concerned some respondents. Including people with certain personality problems was seen as a potential issue by others, because of safeguarding issues, particularly where there are children in the congregation. One commented: "Our openness and welcoming should not prevent us from proper safeguarding, so that our congregations are safe spaces." Another wrote: "There has to be a limit ... this limit is where someone may be so damaging to the congregation that he/she has to be excluded. Many church constitutions/ rules make this point." Other respondents were concerned that Unitarians "do not mistake inclusion and equality for allowing another to abuse our own right to inclusion and equality".

*Chapter 4  Unitarian views on morality; sexuality, gender, and marriage; inclusion and equality*

## *Summary of findings*

In the response to the question "What does morality mean to you as a Unitarian?", more than three-quarters expressed belief in the importance of showing compassion – to ourselves, to others, and to the wider world. Two-thirds believe that morality must be a system of thought or belief to be lived by; three-fifths think it should include respecting the beliefs and life journeys of others, and/or living out the Unitarian values of freedom of belief, based on reason and conscience, accepting the right of others to do the same. Fewer than half believe that it is about being open and inclusive and welcoming to all people, all ideas.

These comments show a deep engagement with the issues: while most are clear that morality involves actions rather than mere words, some take issue with the concepts of respecting the beliefs and life journeys of others, or being welcoming to all people, and all ideas, on the grounds that there is a line to be drawn beyond which certain ideas and behaviours should not be respected or welcomed.

On sexuality and relationships, most share the view of the respondent who wrote: "All human relationships must be based on appreciating the worth and dignity of each other and an absence of exploitation of any kind." Many believe that Unitarians should celebrate diversity, accepting people as people, of whatever gender or sexuality; but others have reservations about the idea of equal marriage. Again, this demonstrates that not all Unitarians have the same views about how liberal the denomination should be about these matters.

While inclusion and equality are highly valued as ideals, and many Unitarian respondents strive to put them into practice, both in their personal lives and in their church and chapel communities, there is still some fear of the stranger among them. More than 80 per cent of respondents chose the options "Everyone is human, and is entitled to equal respect and opportunities" and/or "Our congregations as well as we as individuals need to be open and inclusive and welcoming". Yet some were clear that there need to be limits about how open and inclusive and welcoming Unitarians should, or perhaps even could, be. Certain behaviours and beliefs prompted the definition of personal 'red lines' for respondents beyond which they would not go.

Morality, sexuality, gender, marriage, inclusivity, and equality are big issues that demand careful thought and sensitive action. The responses in this chapter show that Unitarians do engage with these issues. In general this engagement is compassionate, respectful of others, and in line with Unitarian values. But Unitarians ask questions, and their complete acceptance of liberal values cannot automatically be assumed.

## *Questions for reflection or group discussion*

1. *How do your personal morality and your Unitarian values work out in your daily life?*

2. *How important to you is understanding other people's sexuality, gender identity, and relationship diversity?*

3. *How inclusive and welcoming should Unitarian congregations be? Should there be any limits to this?*

# Chapter 5
# *Religion and politics; Earth and the environment; war and peace; and social justice issues*

*Our world is one world:*
*Its ways of wealth affect us all –*
*The way we spend, the way we share,*
*Who are the rich or poor,*
*Who stand or fall?*

Cecily Taylor, Sing Your Faith, 128

This chapter will consider respondents' views on religion and politics, and on particular issues of social justice, such as the environment, and war and peace, and their choices of the issues that they might prioritise, both as individuals and as congregations.

## Unitarian views on religion and politics

Respondents were offered five options for this question:

- Religion and politics should be kept completely separate: religion should not influence politics at any level.
- The moral and ethical values taught by religions should influence politics at all levels.
- Our religious and political views are integral parts of us, so it is inevitable that they will influence each other.

- Deeds not creeds: it is important to put our religious and ethical beliefs into action for social justice.
- Our religious and moral views should help us to live more kindly and generously in the world where we are.

Figure 5.1 shows the choices that respondents made. The only option to attract many participants on its own (24 people: 9 per cent) was the third: the statement that our religious and political views are integral parts of us, so that they inevitably influence each other. Two popular combinations of options were 'Integral parts of us' + 'Deeds not creeds' + 'Should help us to live more kindly' (67: 26 per cent) and a combination of all options except 'They should be separate': 59 (23 per cent). This was a complex question, and respondents' views reflected that fact in the number and range of comments made. These are summarised below.

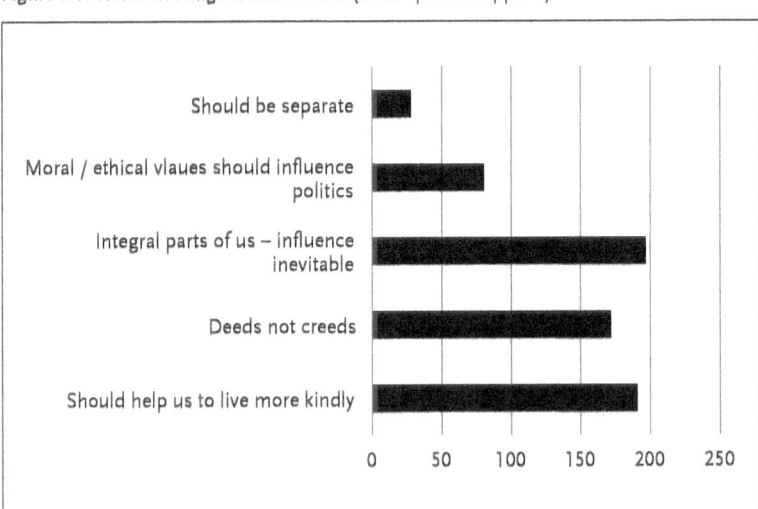

Figure 5.1: Views on Religion and Politics (from options supplied)

## The separation of 'church' and 'state'

Several people believed firmly in the separation of church/ religion and state. One wrote: "The state should be formally secular, with no religion having more privileged access than any other." Another commented: "I am pleased that the Unitarian GA supports the Accord Coalition, which aims to ensure that state education is open to all children regardless of their parents' beliefs. I think that it is entirely consistent with a liberal approach to religious identity."

## Concerns about the influence of politics on religion

Others were concerned about the influence of politics on religion, both collectively and individually. One wrote:

> *Just as we have become over-rational, we have become over-political. Once one removes the transcendent dimension – 'God', 'the soul', 'life after death', 'ultimate purpose' – from a religious movement, politics alone remains. We seem to be at this point, and it is certainly contributing to our demise ... We need to begin a serious exploration of the transcendent.*

Another commented: "I tend to keep them separate – the space on Sundays 'beyond' worldly stuff and a place for respite and renewal of the spirit. ... I also believe true change happens at the spiritual level rather than wholly on the worldly one."

## Caveats about party politics and chapel life

Some respondents were wary of party politics infiltrating chapel life. One wrote: "We must be careful to accept that fellow Unitarians won't always vote as we do, but be ready to discuss issues amicably." Another agreed, commenting: "People should not be judged by their political views. I appreciate that Unitarianism is meant to be non-judgemental, but I often find my politics are in the minority of the congregation and feel scared to share them, even though we purport to be accepting of each other." A third had learned this lesson the hard way: "My political beliefs are very strong, equal to my moral and spiritual beliefs ... I have used my political beliefs to inform my chapel community of campaigns. However, I recently decided to stop, because not everyone agrees ... and I don't want conflict or to feel angry."

### Politics and religion should be influenced by each other
Many respondents believed that politics and faith *are* influenced by each other. One stated firmly: "I am a political person and have been for most of my life. ... My politics and my faith are influenced by each other, and both are very important to me." Another believed: "The two are inseparable, but it must always be kept in mind that there is no such thing as absolute certainty in either." This respondent confirmed this link:

> *My faith informs my daily living, therefore all aspects of my life. My faith therefore informs my political choices. It would be wrong to ask those in politics to do otherwise. This is at a personal level. In government, all voices should be heard, and a democratic process duly observed.*

Others saw a clear link between people's morality and ethics and their political decision making: "Ethics should influence politics, but they need not stem from religion." Another agreed, writing: "Religious views should not influence politics. Shared moral values should." But a third commented: "Our nature as spiritual beings means we will inevitably be shaped by questions of morality in our decision-making".

### Politics and religion should not be influenced by each other
Some respondents were more cautious about the influence of religious views on politics. One gave an example: "We must be careful here. What about religion influencing decisions about sexuality, abortion, women's rights? What about the benefits cap for a woman who has two children, is then raped and becomes pregnant, decides not to have an abortion and then is denied child benefit for the third child she brings up?" Another commented: "Organised creedal religions have exerted a baleful influence in the past of our own country and continue to do so in others round the world."

A third wrote: "I decided not to tick 'should influence politics at all levels' because of course some people attribute really hateful views to their religious teachings, and it appals me when these are used for justification of oppressive politics."

**Should Unitarians speak out collectively on political matters?**
The final issue was whether Unitarians should speak out collectively on political matters. The position of those who believed that political views should be entirely an individual matter may be summarised by the respondent who commented: "This we should practise as individuals. I do not believe that the movement should pontificate or take positions, assuming that it can speak on my behalf." Another agreed, writing: "I do not like religious 'organisations' meddling in politics. They have enough work to do in their primary purpose, inspiring and nurturing the spiritual life and practices of their adherents."

On the other side of the debate were those who believed that Unitarians have a positive duty to speak out as people of faith. One wrote: "As people of faith, it is vital that we speak out at all levels of politics, in order to speak for those who have no voice, no power, nobody campaigning on their behalf. ... Unitarians need to be included as people of faith in politics."

The rest of this chapter will consider respondents' views on the Earth and the environment, on war and peace, and which social-justice issues were important to them.

## *Unitarian views on the Earth and the environment*

Respondents were offered five options to prompt reflection on this theme.

- God created the Earth, and humankind are its stewards.
- The whole of life is inter-connected, inter-woven; therefore we need to be careful of our actions because of their impact on the rest of the world.
- Every living being is sacred, and every place is holy ground; all deserve our respect and reverence.

- We are here to serve and nurture the Earth and her inhabitants, not the other way round.
- I revere the natural world.

The choices that they made are shown in Figure 5.2. The only single option to attract a significant number of votes (18: 19 per cent) was the second: that the whole of life is interconnected. Other popular combinations linked this with other options – notably with all the options except 'God created Earth, we are stewards': 46 (18 per cent). A wide range of views are summarised in the shared comments below.

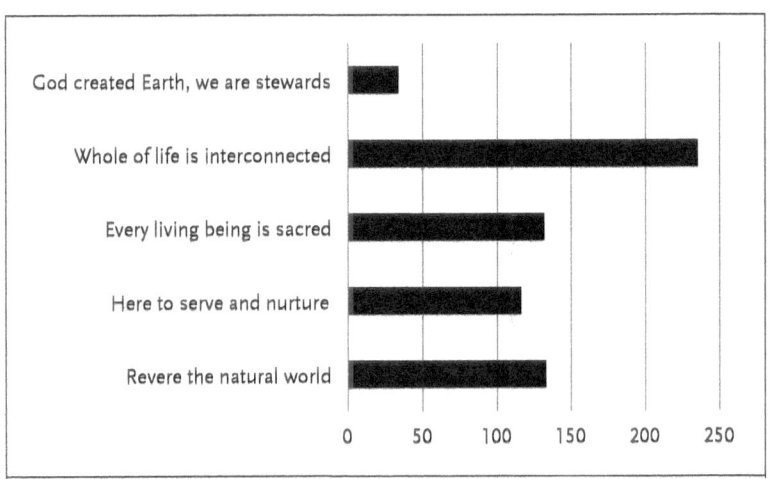

Figure 5.2: Views on the Earth and the environment (from options supplied)

| Option | Value |
|---|---|
| God created Earth, we are stewards | ~30 |
| Whole of life is interconnected | ~235 |
| Every living being is sacred | ~135 |
| Here to serve and nurture | ~115 |
| Revere the natural world | ~135 |

## 'God' and Nature

Some people saw the Earth in terms such as this: "an expression of God's amazing creation and his love". They expressed marvel and awe and wonder "at the beauty and complexity of which we are a part". Others had a more Pagan/Earth Spirit viewpoint. One wrote: "The gods/spirits are emergent properties of the natural world." Another saw "Mother Earth as the Goddess of Creation", while a third wrote: "I am aware that I am more naturally inclined to believe in a sky god than in an earth god – although rationally I see no reason to believe in either reduction of the ultimate unity."

Respondents' views on nature varied. One commented that "Many people find their peace in nature", while another expressed their feeling of being "attuned and connected to the natural world", rather than 'revering' it. A third saw it this way: "Nature is wonderful; it is also harsh. It's a given of which we are a part. Recognising this in an unsentimental way seems to me among the most important aspects of faith."

**Humankind's influence on the natural world/the environment**
Some participants saw humankind as "one species among millions". One wrote: "Humans are not superior to other sentient beings automatically"; and another wrote: "It is a partnership between nature and us." Another explained: "I try to live by *ahimsa* with compassion and non-violence or injury for all living beings (including animals and myself)." For one person, this "needs to include the avoidance of eating meat". Another commented: "We must live in and with the natural world, but not as 'stewards' ordering things to our human ideals, but allowing things to carry on without interference." However, others believed that humankind has a duty and responsibility to care for the Earth and the environment. One person argued:

> *How we treat the planet and the rest of its inhabitants is THE issue of our times. ... There is nothing more important than tackling climate change and global poverty/ inequality. These issues are connected (everything is connected!). We in the West are acting as if nothing we do has any consequences, and whilst those consequences are largely (but not entirely) visited on the developing world, it is all too easy for us to turn our faces away and continue to act irresponsibly. We need to step up to this challenge and be a focus for environmental responsibility and action.*

Another suggested that human beings are

> stewards of the Earth, as to the best of our knowledge we are the species with greatest influence on it. This has become increasingly important as our numbers have burgeoned in recent centuries such that we are decimating other species, causing widespread and damaging pollution of land, sea, and air to our own detriment and that of other living creatures. ... We need to reduce our numbers, through non-coercive means, to a level commensurate with allowing other species to co-exist with us.

Others believed that the most important aim is "to leave the world in a better state than we found it, no matter how small our contribution to that is". One respondent wrote: "I just try my best to respect everything everywhere in every way I can." Another admitted to feeling deeply conflicted: "I would consider myself a hypocrite if I made too many assertions about protecting the environment. I do what I can, but I admit that my lifestyle is less environment-friendly than it could be. But I am not prepared to give up driving my car, putting on the heating, buying fruit and veg out of season, etc."

One person took a strikingly different perspective: "Sometimes I also think that the built environment and social organisations, when they are made with craft and care, are about as precious as a meadow or a skylark, because they are irreplaceable, uplifting, good examples of beauty and the best of humanity, in a world where practical skills are not being learned or valued."

## *Unitarian views on war and peace*

Of all the questions asked in this section of the survey, this was the issue that attracted the widest variety of responses. Participants were offered five options:

- In a world full of conflict, it is vital to stand up for the values of peace, non-violence, and reconciliation.
- Because there is so much conflict and evil in the world, it is sometimes necessary to resort to armed intervention, to prevent a greater evil.
- We are all human beings, all living beings. What right have others to take that away? What cause can possibly justify it?
- It is obscene that so much money is spent on war and violence, when it could be used for alleviating poverty and hunger, improving health and education, protecting the environment, etc.
- It is important to have an effective armed force to defend ourselves and our country.

The choices made by respondents are shown in Figure 5.3. The popular combinations below show the wide range of views on this issue:

- 'Vital to stand up for peace' + 'We are all human beings' + 'Money spent on war is obscene': 43 (17 per cent)
- 'Vital to stand up for peace' + 'Money spent on war is obscene': 34 (13 per cent)
- 'Vital to stand up for peace' + 'Armed intervention sometimes necessary' + 'Money spent on war is obscene' + 'Important to have effective armed force': 31 (12 per cent)

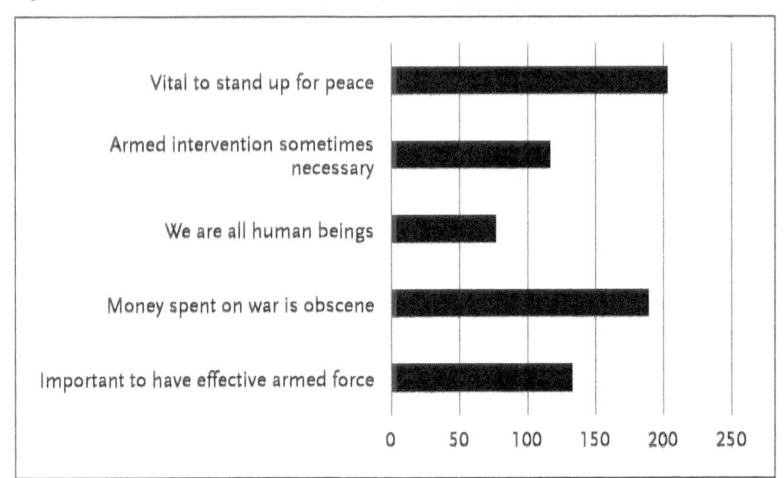

Figure 5.3: Views on War and Peace (from options supplied)

| View | Count |
|---|---|
| Vital to stand up for peace | ~205 |
| Armed intervention sometimes necessary | ~115 |
| We are all human beings | ~75 |
| Money spent on war is obscene | ~190 |
| Important to have effective armed force | ~130 |

Small numbers chose other combinations. It is clear from respondents' choices that Unitarians hold a wide range of views about war and peace. These are summarised below.

### Armed force can be justified for defence or protection

Many respondents agreed that armed force or intervention could be justified for defence or protection purposes; but they often regretted that this was necessary. These two comments are representative of many:

*I'm not a pacifist. I have thought long and hard about it, and I believe that there are times when violence, even killing, are justified in self-defence. That said, I do not support first-strike use of violence, and I oppose all weapons of mass destruction.*

*A difficult question, I feel conflicted. I believe wholeheartedly in peace, yet know I would defend with whatever force necessary those I love. If I love my neighbour, I must admit the need to defend them too.*

## War is sometimes just, necessary, or inevitable

Some people cited World War Two as an example of a just war. One wrote: "I would have been willing to go to war against Hitler – talking and reason failed. I believe that all measures should be taken to avoid conflict, but I could not have been a conscientious objector." Another commented: "I tick this with sadness – thinking back to the overthrow of Hitler – perhaps this was a just war? Which is why I cannot be a full pacifist, even though I am inclined towards this and recognise there are all too many unjust wars." A third simply stated: "I am the daughter of a political refugee, who escaped from Nazi Germany."

One respondent quoted the political theorist and philosopher Edmund Burke: "For evil to triumph it is merely necessary for good people to do nothing." Another argued that "Conflict, and therefore war, is part of nature. It's not necessarily a matter of good and evil, but of the struggle for survival. Miscalculation can lead to war, so clear signals by all parties are important. By the use of reason and diplomacy wars can often be avoided, but not, in the nature of things, always. I think we should be less moralistic about war."

Some participants commented about the inevitability of war while inequality exists. One wrote: "Human beings are creatively destructive in their quest to acquire resources, which in turn gives them power over others. While there is inequity, there cannot be justice, and without justice, war is inevitable."

## The role of the United Kingdom in the world

Several people commented about the role of the United Kingdom in the world. One wrote: "It is important to step practically and safely from our 'armed to the teeth' mindset to a token military. We can only do this safely by being less belligerent on the world stage." Another agreed, commenting: "As a nation we must avoid the hubris of believing we have a status greater than the reality and adapt our policies accordingly, for example balancing defence against our health and social-welfare budget."

One respondent believed that the United Kingdom "should be a non-aligned country, pledged to use its military forces only in self-defence and for peace-keeping/ peace-making operations under the UN/NATO/EU". Another agreed, adding "It is important to have effective armed forces in the UK, in order to work together with other democratic countries, to protect people in other parts of the world who have nobody to look after them."

Two others spoke out against the United Kingdom's nuclear capability. One asked: "So many other countries don't have them, why should we?" The other was more outspoken, commenting: "The recent terrorist atrocity in Manchester has (yet again) demonstrated just how irrelevant Trident is to our defences. While I agree we need to defend ourselves, I do not think we are going the right way about doing it, and the ludicrously expensive sacred cow of nuclear weapons needs to be ditched, because we can't afford it, we couldn't use it (I hope!), and it DOESN'T EVEN WORK." But another disagreed, writing: "I do believe that nuclear weapons have been a deterrent."

### Peace-keeping and conflict resolution
One person commented in favour of a peace-keeping role: "Peace-keeping must be seen as both short-term and long-term strategy, and therefore requires a greater degree of investment than we often presume." Others mentioned the importance of conflict resolution: "I think that conflict is a naturally occurring thing in humans. It's finding ways to manage conflicts and find workable and sustaining solutions which I think is important." Another added: "Recognition of the methods and place of conflict resolution has increased within our movement, but could be strengthened."

### The necessity of working for peace
Some respondents reflected on the need to work for peace in the world. One wrote: "I cannot envisage peace between the nations of the world – many want what others have, many want to impose their own beliefs (political and religious). ... I feel we can only work towards resolving the underlying problems – but I do not believe we will be successful. Yet I am hopeful!"

Two others suggested ways of working for peace. One wrote: "In a world where violent conflict exists, it is vital to continually interrogate our values of peace and work with other faiths, cultures, and organisations, governments and industry to promote mutual understanding and commonality." Another commented: "Working for peace is absolutely vital, but it should be done 'upstream' in promoting mutual tolerance and understanding between human tribes, and not 'downstream' in potentially dangerous disarmament." Some suggested that working for peace could be a spiritual practice. One wrote:

> *We can both preach and practise alternatives to fighting such as peacemaking, active listening, and non-violent non-cooperation with evil. We can preach and practise kindness, empathy, emotional intelligence, respect/ tolerance, and other peaceable virtues. And we can most fundamentally live by aligning ourselves with Spirit more and ego less. These spiritual thoughts and actions are the contribution that Unitarians and other faiths can with integrity make towards humanity continuing and accelerating its movement in a peaceable direction.*

## *Unitarian views on issues of social justice*

The final question in this section of the survey asked respondents "Which social justice issues should be a priority for Unitarians?" They were asked to tick up to three options from the following:

- Animal rights
- Environmental issues
- Penal affairs, prisoners of conscience
- LGBTQIA+ issues
- Peace work
- Developing world/refugees

The options chosen are shown in Figure 5.4. The most common combinations were 'Environmental issues' + other issues, the most popular being 'Environmental issues' + 'Peace work' + 'Developing world/ refugees':

38 (15 per cent). Twenty-one (8 per cent) refused to choose any options at all, as they did not consider this an appropriate way of thinking about issues of social justice. The further views of respondents are summarised in the shared comments below.

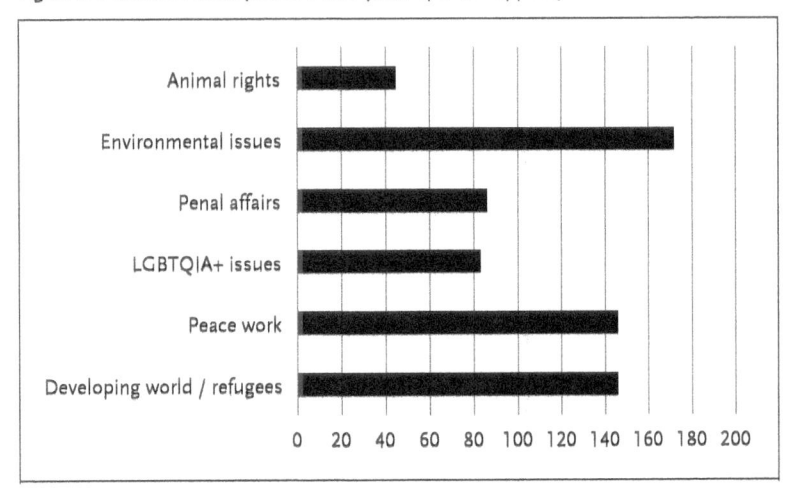

Figure 5.4: Views on social justice issues (from options supplied)

| Issue | Count |
|---|---|
| Animal rights | ~45 |
| Environmental issues | ~170 |
| Penal affairs | ~85 |
| LGBTQIA+ issues | ~85 |
| Peace work | ~145 |
| Developing world / refugees | ~150 |

### Choice should be at the individual or local level

Although the intention of the question had been to discover which social-justice issues participants believed were most important to them as individuals, the wording of it was often interpreted to mean "Which social-justice issues should the national movement unite behind?" Naturally, a significant number of people were not happy with this idea. Others insisted on their individual right to choose which social-justice issues were important to them. This quotation perhaps encapsulates the point: "Each Unitarian for whom social action is a priority does well to involve herself or himself with any social action that appeals to them personally by working with the charity or campaign that specialises in their issue of choice."

## Inequality, discrimination, poverty, deprivation, homelessness

Of the 'other' issues listed by respondents, the related issues of inequality, discrimination, poverty, and social deprivation were the most frequently mentioned. One summed it up as follows: "Addressing inequality, poverty, and marginalisation of all vulnerable people and improving access to resources for everyone". Others mentioned "disadvantaged UK families, especially children" and "issues to do with groups who are isolated/ dropping through safety nets in the UK (disabled, mental health, ageing)".

Homelessness and housing problems were also cited by several people, often in conjunction with the issues of social deprivation listed above. One wrote: "Everyone needs a space to call home." Others mentioned "Mental, physical and social health: to take a holistic approach". These issues were often perceived as priorities in the context of the local community. One respondent commented: "Important to develop help for these issues which are presenting locally, everyday problems which burden people." Another suggested "issues of support for those in need that directly involve the communities in which we live".

## Inter-faith understanding

Some participants thought that the obvious core cause for Unitarians to adopt would be inter-faith understanding, working to improve relations between faith communities. One commented: "I accept that there is tension between being proactive in this area and at the same time becoming more aware of times when we might need to challenge certain practices or beliefs that we see as harmful. But to me this is something that we should see as a logical consequence of our standpoint, and a service we can and should face up to, developing our skills and knowledge. ... Community cohesion is a fragile thing, and anything we can do to help would seem worthwhile."

## How to prioritise; reasons for choosing particular issues

Some people shared their reasons for choosing particular options. One commented: "I've chosen LGBT etc issues because it's an area in which the Unitarians have a record to be proud of ... I've also selected the developing world/ refugees because it is against these countries and people that so much hatred is generated. Any religious group that says it stands for compassion has to stand with refugees, and be bold about it." Another wrote: "All are important, but I think that environmental issues are now the priorities."

## *Summary of findings*

The interplay between political priorities, ethics and moral values, and religious and spiritual beliefs is very complex, and respondents' views reflected this complexity. More than three-quarters of the participants believe them all to be integral parts of being human, making mutual influence inevitable; and/or they believe that "our religious and moral views should help us to live more kindly and generously in the world where we are". Another two-thirds chose the option "Deeds not creeds – it is important to put our religious and ethical beliefs into action for social justice". Slightly fewer than one third believe that "the moral and ethical values taught by religions should influence politics at all levels".

Some are concerned about the influence of politics on religion, both collectively and individually. Conversely, others are concerned about the influence of some religious views on political and moral issues. Many believe that the influence of the one on the other is inevitable, with varying results. Some are wary of the infiltration of party politics into chapel life; those whose views are different from the majority of the congregation sometimes feel judged.

By far the most popular option for the question "What are your views on the Earth/ the environment?" was "The whole of life is inter-connected, inter-woven; therefore we need to be careful of our actions because of their impact on the rest of the world", which was chosen by more than 90 per cent of respondents. Three other options attracted substantial support. The comments show a great deal of care and reverence for the natural world, whether it is perceived as a creation of the Divine, or as a set of purely natural phenomena. This was accompanied by a deep concern for the impact that human actions are having on the planet.

All respondents would rather advocate peace, but many believe that conflict and war are inevitable parts of the world in its current state, and that it is often necessary to used armed force, both for defensive purposes and to intervene where others are being oppressed. Some reflected on the role of the United Kingdom on the world stage, mainly advocating defensive or peace-keeping roles. Working for peace is seen by some to be a spiritual practice.

There is a clear and well-articulated commitment to a range of social-justice issues, but a caveat that these should be very much determined by the individual, and that often they will reflect local needs. A small minority wrote that there might be occasions and issues when Unitarians as a body might speak out collectively.

## *Questions for reflection or group discussion*

1. What is the relationship between religion and politics in your life?

2. If the whole of life is interconnected, what can we do to support our planet and its inhabitants?

# Chapter 6
# Unitarian perspectives on divinity

*Our true God we there shall find*
*In what claims our heart and mind,*
*And our hidden thoughts enshrine*
*That which for us is Divine.*

John Andrew Storey, *Hymns for Living*, 35

This is one of several issues in the survey for which respondents were not given any options to choose from. In this instance, they were asked instead:

*The Divine can mean God, Goddess, the Universe, or however you perceive that which is greater than humankind. In a few sentences, please describe your perspectives on divinity.*

There was a wide range of responses, which may be divided into four very broad categories, each of which will be covered in this chapter:

- Responses about the nature of God/the Divine
- Responses about the Ground of All Being/Force for Good
- Responses relating the Divine to humankind
- Other responses.

## *The nature of God/the Divine*

A small number of people struggled with the language. One wrote: "Personal difficulty with the word God, having been brought up in Anglo-Catholic 'dystopian' frenzy for the wicked." Another commented: "Not sure, that's why I go to Unitarian church. I can certainly say that I'm not comfortable calling God 'Lord'. Prefer terms like 'The Spirit of Life/of Love', 'The Unifying Spirit', 'Holy Spirit', 'Universal Father/ Mother/ Parent'." One wrote simply: "God is God". Another saw God as "my Higher Power. I cannot picture how this Higher Power looks, but I know it is with me all of the time."

### The qualities of God/the Divine

The idea of the immanence and/or transcendence of the Divine was addressed by many. Some believed in a transcendent divinity. One wrote: "God is beyond not only gender and flesh, but also time and intention. It's very abstract." Another commented: "Whatever it is, the divine is the essence of otherness, and what we do is to try to use metaphors to work it into our lives ... I must have a commitment somewhere, a trust, that this is all worth it, that we are more than the sum of our parts, and yes, I feel and have felt that I am held in the hand of God – so lightly, but so well." Others disagreed, and one wrote: "I do not believe [in] a supernatural reality beyond this world. I do not believe in a God 'up there' or 'out there'."

Some participants did not use the word 'transcendence', but perceived the Divine to be "that which is greater than humankind". One wrote: "I would define God as some greater force than ourselves." Another commented: "Divinity to me is within us all, but greater than us all. It is the sum of the good and holy within us that creates an unknown entity."

Many people perceived God/the Divine as an immanent presence within all human beings. Their comments included some thoughtful reflections, such as this one: "I conclude that 'the Divine' exists within each one of us, prompting us to standards of morality, to care for our fellow beings and to try to leave the world a better place than we found it." Another believed God to be "that creative, inspiring, loving presence working in me, through me, around me – and sometimes despite me".

Others perceived the Divine as both transcendent and immanent. One wrote: "He/She is both infinitely greater and other than us, but also the very deepest part of our being." One sensed it as "always present and also far away". One respondent wrote: "I don't worship a God I cannot see, but I do see God in every person I meet." Another wrote: "Because God is everywhere and flows through us all, I believe it is possible for us to have a personal connection with God when we reach deep into ourselves." Some described the Divine as "ineffable and eternal". One wrote: "The Divine can be perceived, but not understood – it can inspire." Others found the Divine in "that which is sacred, most holy, most worthy of honour" ... "that which is of ultimate worth".

### God/the Divine at the centre of all things

For some respondents, God, as they perceived Him/Her/It, was of central importance in their lives. One wrote: "Emotionally I feel in deep relationship with something I choose to call God. This is the central relationship of my life, on which all my other relationships are based." Another believed: "The divine is that in which we 'live and move and have our being'." One person wrote:

> *The Divine is infinite, everywhere, omniscient, omnipotent, and all loving. It is within me, and you, and everyone else, and all creatures, plants, rocks, rivers, and the deep salt sea which surrounds and connects us all. All particles, quanta, universes (dark or otherwise, composed of matter or otherwise), thoughts, feelings, consciousness, and experiences are within the Divine. The Divine is also more than all this, more than its Creation, more than I or any mortal mind can conceive. The Divine is the true Reality.*

This panentheist viewpoint was shared by many participants. One wrote simply: "Everything is infused with the Divine." Another saw the Divine in these terms:

> That which is within and that which connects me to the whole, as well as
> all that is. There is lack of separation and division when spirit speaks to
> spirit. It is God within, the God between and God the other. The Divine is
> the breath shared between me and creation. The Divine is wholeness. The
> Divine is the eternal energy of the world that flows through all. The Divine
> is Love. Without the Divine of many names, there is no meaningful life.

One person described it as "A benevolent spirit which is within all things, much like the Chinese concept of the Tao. We can choose to worship this force in the form of any goddess or god, because it is a spirit of infinite possibility."

### God/the Divine in the natural world
One respondent commented: "I look to nature for a sense of the Divine." A fuller perception was shared by another: "My idea of God is the evolving blueprint of Nature, in microcosm and macrocosm – from cells to stars. This God is not personal, or nationalistic, nor served by one, or any, religion, and cannot intervene in human affairs, or animal survival or extinction." A third stated: "Gaia. The living planet is the most important thing – I would not use the word god or divine here."

### God/the Divine as Love
Some saw the Divine simply as Love, whether this was 'God as Love' or 'God as the love between and within people'. One person wrote: "Divinity for me is a loving energy which connects us all. ... I feel that it holds me in my life as it holds everyone and all life. I do not 'believe' in it so much as experience and feel it. It is immeasurable Love and endless Compassion." Another described it as "the Spirit of Peace, Truth and Love". A third suggested that "The Divine ... gives protection, direction and love". One person suggested: "It is possible to have experiences of the Divine ... a great love that exists and is personal ... is accessible to all humankind." Another wrote of "the spark which creates life in all its forms, and which in some way inspires us (and perhaps other life forms) to respond to life and creation with wonder, joy, compassion, love and further creativity".

### The nature of Jesus
Some respondents commented on the nature of Jesus. One wrote: "Jesus was not divine or God or Holy Trinity." Another commented: "I still have no idea of God – just a feeling. But I cling to the teachings of our Elder Brother Jesus to keep me thinking and acting in the Way, and for allowing me glimpses of God – enough to sustain my belief, and that I am still on the Path."

## *The Ground of All Being/Force for Good*

Most of the respondents quoted in the previous section saw the Divine in some way "personified". Here there is a less personal perception of what the Divine means.

### The Divine a force for Good
Some people saw the Divine as "a force for the good; benign, creative energy". One described it as "A pure, positive energy, nurturing, non-judgemental, inclusive and the pure force of life itself. It flows through everything in different frequencies." Another called it "The unseen, unknowable wonder which keeps the entire universe from the vast to the infinitesimal interconnected and active". A few wrote of being able to tap into this force in some way: "I see a continuously flowing river of energy and creativity, into which I am able to tap, which rejuvenates me and re-commits me to living in its precious waters." Another described it as "A great source of joy, strength, wonder and mystery". A third perceived it as "a universal energy which has a power and a depth to it which we can never really express but can sometimes feel or connect with".

### The Divine as mystery
Some participants expressed their sense of the Divine in words such as "the Mystery beyond our words to express but not beyond our lives to experience". Another suggested: "Our journey is about encountering, embracing and living with that [mystery] as we attempt to understand where we are on our respective journeys." This was echoed by another,

who wrote: "How the universe exists is a mystery and a cause for wonder. Planet Earth itself is far greater than humankind." Another commented: "The divine is ultimately unknowable, may exist in a different form beyond what we think we know about existence."

### The Divine as source/ground of being

For others, the Divine is the source of all being. One respondent explained: "God is 'What is': when we are born, we come out of 'What is', and when we die we return home. The thread of God that is me is self-aware, and my life is part of the overall tapestry in which we make connections and relationships which continue after death when we are re-absorbed into 'What is'." This was echoed by another, who wrote: "I believe in a deity who is the wellspring of everything, the ground and source of existence, and I believe that this wellspring is loving and can be defined as love itself." Another had a different perspective on

> *the 'Ground of all being' idea of divinity; a sort of enabling condition for all existence. A metaphor which works for me [is] the universe being like a beautifully worked needlepoint cushion; what you can't see is the canvas underneath, on to which the whole thing has been worked and without which all you'd have is a random, meaningless tangle of threads of wool. So my God is non-interventionist, not a superman with a plan, not a Creator. ... But without God, nothing.*

## *The Divine and humankind*

A third group of respondents found their sense of the Divine in relation to humankind.

### The Divine as humankind's search for meaning

Several used the concept of the Divine "not as applying to a spirit, but as an amalgam of meanings attached to our daily living". One wrote: "I am confident that Man made God in his own image, not the other way round." Another commented: "The essence of our being is that we are living, thinking beings: we are self-aware, with the capacity for love and compassion, to perform great things but also terrible things. That said, we are fully able to choose which. I believe that the Divine lies within our subjective experience of reality." In other words, "What we call God is a construct of ours to help us explain the mystery of our very existence." Continuing this thread, another respondent wrote: "My view of the 'divine' is that it is humankind's search for meaning in their lives and the need to understand their existence. I don't believe in a God in human form, the divine for me is within people. ... I believe all is rooted in human psychology, a need for meaning, morals, ethics to live by, reward for a life lived well, forgiveness for mistakes and wrongdoing."

### The Divine as humankind's spiritual aspiration

One person wrote: "The notion of the divine is an aspect of our spiritual aspiration. It is a mental concept that has no other existence apart from our longing to reach beyond ourselves. Our sense of divinity is an aspect of our self-awareness. Outside the human mind, divinity has no existence." Another expressed a similar view: "I think it's about what's sacred and of most value to people and what aids us in bringing out the best in us and helping us to lead the best lives for ourselves and to benefit others. And that may be the 'divinity of humankind' for some." For some, the Divine is "A spiritual quality, a plus factor, an added dimension to human experience. It is to be found in personal relationships, when persons establish a loving rapport. It is found in community spirit. It is found in our relationship with creation. ... The Divine is relationships."

### The Divine as a function of human consciousness

Other participants saw the Divine as a function of human consciousness. One person wrote of it this way:

> *The divine as a concept ... manifests to me in those transformative moments which somehow light up the best, the possible, the wondrous, and lift us out of the mundane. A phenomenon of the mystery of*

*consciousness, usually involving connection between myself and others, or myself and nature. Or involving a situation which has been transformed, turned round, by the skills, love, and/or special gifts of a person of goodwill, often against the odds.*

Another respondent wrote: "Consciousness is the function of the whole person in the intersubjective relations in the environing world. ... God can be understood as the process through which this is made possible."

### The Divine as manifested in the good qualities of people

Some perceived the presence of God/the Divine in "the love between people". One wrote: "I see glimpses of it in the love between human beings." Another commented: "I see it mostly in the goodness of other people, some of whom might never have entered a church." A third believed: "There is a possibility of a deep spiritual connection between people who enter into prayer together." A fourth found their concept of the Divine in "The very best of the human spirit, kindness, goodness, thoughtfulness, selflessness". Some saw this "very best of the human spirit" as manifested in "a leader, a teacher, an example to model one's life on, regardless of faith and religion".

One respondent offered a "Buddhist Unitarian" perspective on divinity. "I find God in nature and in us, by extension, but have never been able to pray to God or feel that it is a moral being who demands praise or has any kind of plan for me. I am a Buddhist who follows the advice of the Buddha about how to live my life and the attitudes to take to things like impermanence. I don't find it too difficult to call myself a Buddhist Unitarian."

## *Other responses*

The final group of respondents either rejected the concept of the Divine or were uncertain or open-minded about it.

## Agnostic responses

One person wrote: "I don't know and I don't mind that I don't know. There is a freedom in that. ... God is what we call that which we don't yet understand." Another admitted: "Divinity is a concept that I do not fully understand. ... We all like to think there is something in life which is on a higher and perhaps less worldly plane than we are on ourselves. Whether we have created this divinity I am not sure." A third commented: "God is so far beyond my understanding that even if the words existed I would still be unable to explain the unique, elemental, unknowable source of that which we call God." Another called the Divine "That 'presence' which cannot be named. Language is quite inadequate, but metaphor sometimes works. Some of the Eastern religions point the way." A third wrote simply: "The divine is not describable for me – it is all and everything."

Others freely admitted that their beliefs about the Divine were not fixed. One wrote: "I am agnostic about this question, but find materialism also leaves questions unanswered." Another commented: "My views have changed and are still changing – and I am pleased about this, as I feel, as a human, I have no need for a final answer, and Love is a vital component. I use God, Goddess, the Universe, Life, Higher Power, the Tao, Nature, at different times, depending on who I am with."

## Atheist responses

Some respondents rejected the concept of the Divine altogether, taking an atheist perspective, as in these two comments: "Divinity is entirely irrelevant to my way of life" and "no concept of anything that exists that has influence on human activity other than the natural forces of the material universe". Others believed that God/ the Divine is a human creation. One commented: "There is no such thing as 'the Divine'. Every person has her/his own idea of what is 'divine' for them. It is not something outside ourselves. It is how we see things. Humankind is just one part of existence. There is nothing 'greater' than what exists." Another wrote: "All gods are human creations."

## *Summary of findings*

The responses to this question were varied, sometimes complex, and spanned the whole theological spectrum. Those who believe in a personal God or divinity commented on the nature of this God, invoking such qualities as transcendence, immanence, ineffability, and omnipotence. They also shared their beliefs in the Divine as the centre of all things, or as a presence in the natural world, or as love, whether this is 'God as Love' or 'God as the love between and within people'. Others have a less personal perception of what the Divine means to them, perceiving it to be a force for good, or a mystery, or as the source or ground of being.

A third group find their perception of the Divine in the best aspects of humankind, embodied in people's search for meaning, their spiritual aspirations, their good qualities, or as a function of human consciousness. Another group are not sure whether any Divine being exists. Some admit that their ideas on the subject are not fixed, while others believe that language is inadequate to describe their beliefs. Some reject the concept of the Divine entirely, taking an atheist perspective.

The 257 respondents to the questionnaire exhibited a wide range of views and many different ways of expressing these views. It seems likely that this spread of ideas on the nature of the Divine is replicated in the Unitarian movement as a whole. At a single congregational level there may be a more focused range of views, for many reasons, social and historical; but this may well change over time as the congregation changes and develops. For the individual Unitarian, perhaps the matter is best summed up by the widely respected hymn writer John Storey, in the hymn quoted at the beginning of this chapter:

*Though the truth we can't perceive,*
*This at least we must believe,*
*What we take most earnestly*
*Is our living Deity.*

## *Question for reflection or group discussion*

1. *What is your own perspective on 'divinity'?*

# Chapter 7
# Unitarians' relationship with Christianity

*Long ago in sacred silence*
*Died the accents of his prayer;*
*Still the souls that seek God's spirit*
*Find that presence everywhere.*

From William George Tarrant, *Hymns for Living*, 100

The fifth section of the survey was concerned with Unitarian and Free Christian relationships with Christianity, the religious tradition from which the present-day Unitarian movement has evolved. The next two chapters will address this theme. In this chapter, the following questions will be considered:

- What do you believe about Jesus?
- How would you describe the Holy Spirit?
- What are your views about the doctrine of the Trinity?
- What do you believe about the Bible?

## Unitarian beliefs about Jesus

For Christians, Jesus is of central importance. He is the divine Son of God, Second Person of the Trinity, who died that they might be in right relationship with God the Father. Unitarians hold somewhat different views. Respondents were offered six options for this question:

- He is the Son of God, second Person of the Trinity.
- He was a son of God, in the same way that we are all sons and daughters of God.
- He was an entirely human first-century Jewish prophet, whose teachings were/ are inspirational.
- His teaching and example are more important than his death/ resurrection and miracles.
- The story/man Jesus is irrelevant to my beliefs/spirituality.
- He was a mythical figure.

The choices made by respondents are shown in Figure 7.1. The two most popular combinations of options were:

- 'A son of God' + 'Human first-century Jewish prophet' + 'Teachings, example more important' (73: 28 per cent)
- 'Human first-century Jewish prophet' + 'Teachings, example more important' (59: 23 per cent)

Figure 7.1: Beliefs about Jesus (from options supplied)

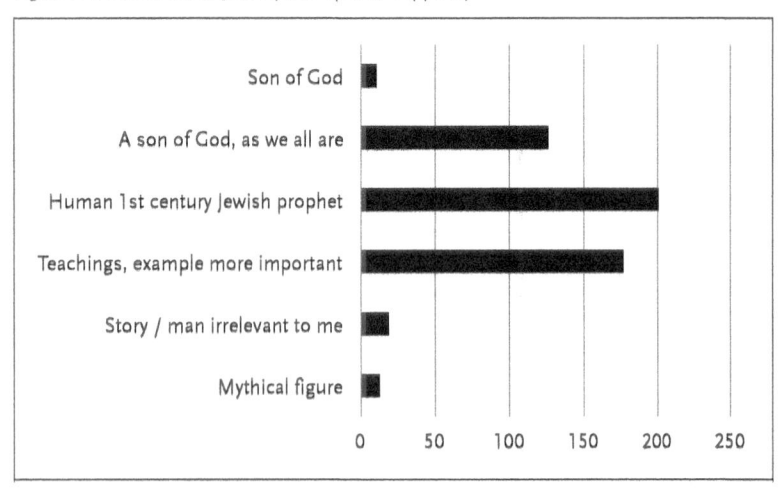

The other respondents chose different combinations of options, but only a small number opted for each combination. Comparatively few people made comments about this question. They are summarised below.

### Jesus more than human/all that we understand about the Divine

One participant believed that "All that we understand about the divine comes from Jesus' life and teaching". Another commented: "He was as we are, but ... manifesting most clearly the divine presence – not the only one – but someone for us to follow and emulate." One person saw Jesus in these terms: "A human who became more than human – in the sense that an avatar in Hindu tradition or a Bodhisattva in Buddhism incarnates in human form, but lives on in some way to help/guide humanity towards enlightenment." Another participant wrote: "I don't have a problem with the possibility that Jesus did perform miracles – as some modern-day gurus and healers seem able to do – there are scientifically verifiable studies which suggest that miracles are natural laws not yet fully understood. To me Jesus is more than just a teacher: he was an archetypal healer – of bodies, minds and spirits."

### Jesus the human prophet and teacher

Concerning the role of Jesus as a human prophet and teacher, three people had comments to make. One wrote: "Jesus was a human being with inspirational teaching, like many before him and many after him. Many inspirational teachers (especially women) have simply never had their teachings noted down. Jesus isn't irrelevant to my beliefs, but he is not more relevant than anyone else who teaches moral lessons that challenge us to bring about a just world." Another commented that, having been brought up in the Jewish tradition, "Christianity is not very relevant to me, apart from respecting Jesus as a great teacher." The third person argued that his teachings have been "often distorted by the Christian church".

### Jesus' death, resurrection, and miracles

Some people asserted that the more supernatural elements of Jesus' life and death were crucial to his message. One wrote: "We wouldn't have the teachings if we didn't have the accompanying miracle stories." Another stated: "I can't separate out his teachings as more important than his death; his being willing to go to his death because of his beliefs makes him more of an inspiration – and the metaphorical message found in the resurrection story is compelling (i.e. love cannot be defeated)." Another partly agreed: "His death is important. His resurrection and miracles are not, for me." Another respondent stated firmly: "I do not believe he was resurrected. That is a myth."

### Jesus the 'mythical' figure

One respondent ticked the second, third, and fourth options, but also commented: "I am also open to the fact that he may have been a mythical figure, and if this is so, it still doesn't detract from the message, it just illustrates it." Another also thought that Jesus might have been mythical, but added: "I do believe that he exists as an entity/ bodhisattva to whom we can pray." Others used phrases such as "spiritual Master" to describe the mythical figure of Jesus. One participant wanted to tick the 'Mythical figure' box "as I find that Biblical Christianity has become less and less important to my spiritual life. However there is undoubtedly a residual effect from years of Christian worship. I respect Christian scripture and sometimes turn to the wisdom found there, but I find myself more often turning to contemporary poets, mystics, and thinkers for my religious, moral, and spiritual inspiration."

## *Unitarian beliefs about the (Holy) Spirit*

The next question asked respondents how they would describe the Holy Spirit. For Christians, this is the Third Person of the Trinity, "God within us", a central concept of Christianity. To prompt reflection, six options were offered:

- The pre-existent, eternal Third Person of the Trinity.
- The Divine breath that "inspires" us with Life.

- The divine spark of God that dwells within each human being, "that of God in everyone".
- The Divine Feminine/Goddess.
- The "Divine DNA" that is present in every living thing, not just human beings.
- The Holy Spirit is irrelevant to my beliefs/spirituality.

The choices made by respondents are shown in Figure 7.2. Two single and contrasting options attracted a significant number of votes: 'Irrelevant to me' (57: 22 per cent); and 'Divine Spark within' (43: 17 per cent). Popular combinations of options were two or three of 'Divine Breath', 'Divine Spark within', and 'Divine DNA in all things'. Others made different choices, but only a small number opted for each combination. This question attracted many comments, the main categories of which are summarised below.

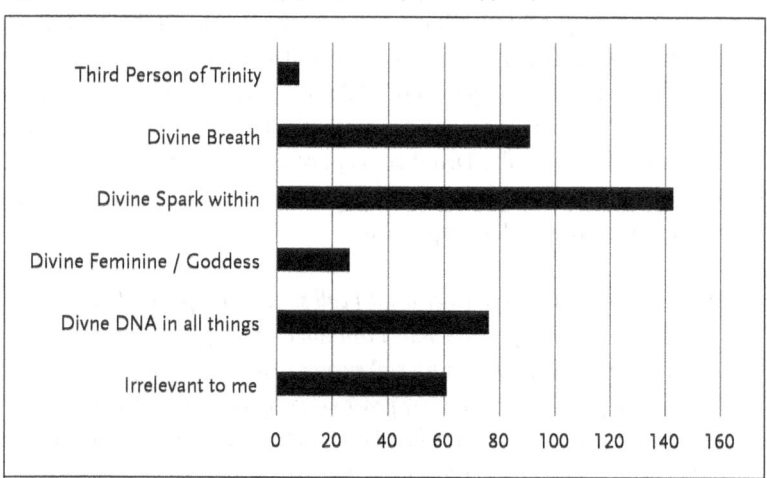

Figure 7.2: Beliefs about the Holy Spirit (from options supplied)

## [Holy] Spirit synonymous with God

Some respondents perceived 'God' and '[Holy] Spirit' to be one and the same. One wrote: "I use the terms God and Spirit interchangeably – I don't perceive them to be two different things." Another wrote simply: "The Holy Spirit is in no way separate from God." A third commented: "My ideas of Spirit and God often merge together, as Cliff Reed[17] has said."

Another saw them as synonymous in a slightly different way: "It doesn't exist in the way that's implicit in these options. Yes, the Divine is Spirit, and is holy. Yes, the Divine is feminine, is present in every living thing, is a 'spark' in everyone, is the Life in us, and is pre-existent (exists outwith time). And the Divine is a Unity, including all this and more, and is more than anyone can conceive with a limited human mind. 'Holy' and 'spirit' are aspects of the whole, not separable components."

One person described the Holy Spirit as "The comforting and sometimes discomforting presence of truth which Jesus promised". Another perceived it as a "source of divine grace and comfort".

### Holy Spirit as the Divine working through us, and in the world

Other participants perceived the Spirit as "The spirit of life which empowers me to action and good living". One commented: "The Holy Spirit is to human beings what my daily thoughts and consciousness are to the individual cells that make up my body." Another wrote of it as "that aspect of the Creative Power that speaks directly to the human soul or psyche". A third identified it with "the Druid concept of the Awen; the inspirational life force which encourages us to live life to the full and be creative and expressive". One respondent explained:

> All I can say is that I experience what I call spirit in prayer, meditation, but also as a constant presence that I can call on at any time to guide me to a better response. It's a very real energy, and I can feel myself move from a place of ego to a more generous perspective when I 'tune in'. ... I also experience Spirit when I communicate well: I used to teach, and sometimes knew I was being inspirational – or rather something inspirational was coming through me to my students.

---

17 Author of *Unitarian? What's That?: Questrions and Answers About a Liberal Religious Alternative* (Lindsey Press, 1999, revised 2018).

Another wrote: "There is something which speaks to us on rare occasions which is moving and memorable, but we cannot know what that is ... one's subconscious mind or some divine presence. ... I find the idea of a divine presence comforting and inspiring ... and if it helps me to live a less self-centred life, then it is a force for good to indulge in that idea of the divine." Perhaps it is, at its most basic, "the creative force beyond human perception".

### Holy Spirit as the Indwelling Presence

Some people perceived an 'Indwelling Presence'. One person called it "the 'Divine DNA' that is present in every sentient being". Another went further, commenting: "I see the Spirit as something a bit like the force, in that it links us and can grow in community and is linked to the rocks and earth and elements of life, as well as all conscious beings and plants and trees."

### Holy Spirit as Sophia, the divine wisdom, the Divine Feminine

One respondent described it as "Sophia, the divine wisdom, an ordering principle in the universe". Another saw it as "The divine feminine principle to 'balance' the Jesus figure (who represents the divine male principle in this case). In my view, much of Christianity was stolen from the prevailing pagan beliefs at the time (as well as the Jewish mythology contained in the Old Testament), and this was the best they could do to represent the female goddess as well as deifying the Virgin Mary."

### Other definitions

Some other participants had their own nuanced definitions of the Holy Spirit, including "The Christian's way to build bridges to other faith traditions, both goddess-honouring and not. It's the only part of the Trinity I can relate to in any spiritually important way." Another saw it as "the 'Cosmic Principle' of Taoism", and a third perceived it as "The awareness which is so difficult to achieve, of our ultimate vulnerability and transience, both individually and communally".

**'Holy Spirit' not a useful or relevant term**
For some respondents, it was not a useful term. One wrote: "Holy spirit isn't a phrase or idea that resonates with me." Another commented: "The term 'Holy Spirit' was only ever used in conjunction with the Trinity, and to me as a Unitarian Christian it really is an irrelevant theological term." Another commented: "I like the idea of a holy spirit as a metaphor, but do not believe in the existence of some separate personification of God. If I believed in the Trinity, I'd be a Trinitarian/ Christian, not a Unitarian!"

## *Unitarian beliefs about the Trinity*

The Christian doctrine of the Trinity holds that God is somehow Three Persons in One: Father, Son, and Holy Spirit. Each of the three Persons is equal in status to the other. The Unitarian faith began to spread when the Bible was translated into the vernacular at the time of the Reformation, as people could read the Bible for themselves, and discovered that the Trinity was not taught therein. However, for many years, Unitarians continued to believe that Jesus was the divine Son of God, but not equal in status to God the Father. Today, Unitarian perspectives on the Trinity are rather different. Respondents to the questionnaire were given the following options:

- It's a useful way of approaching the mystery that is God.
- It represents the flow of love between God, humankind, and all creation.
- I don't believe in the concept of the Trinity.
- I can understand the idea of God being both transcendent ("out there") and immanent ("in our hearts") but struggle with the concept of Jesus' unique divinity. [Referred to as 'Binitarian' in Figure 7.3.]
- It is not relevant to my beliefs/spirituality.
- I do not understand it.

The responses are presented in Figure 7.3. For this question, two of the single options attracted a significant number of votes: 'Do not believe' and 'Not relevant' (28: 11 per cent each). A further 44 (17 per cent) chose both of these. The remaining respondents chose a variety of different options, but only a small number opted for any particular combination. Very few participants commented on this question; their views are summarised in the comments below.

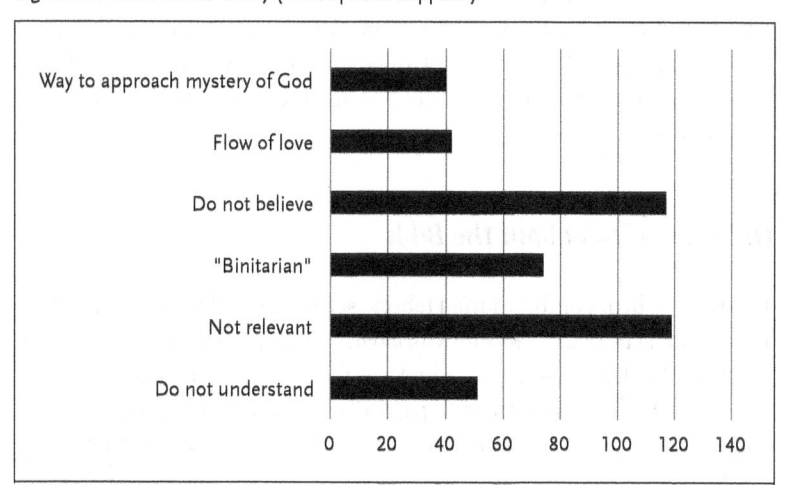

Figure 7.3: Views on the Trinity (from options supplied)

### The Trinity as a human construct
One person called it "A human model of understanding different elements of what we mean by the divine that is useful for many people... but it is one of many models, so if it expands people's thinking that's great, but if it limits it, that's not so good." Another noted: "There are Trinities in other religions that represent the different aspects of God." Another respondent, giving some historical context, wrote that it had been "introduced at the Council of Nicaea in 325 CE as a response to Emperor Constantine's insistence on one set of practical policies and procedures ... so that he could operate Christianity as a unifying force within the Roman Empire".

**The Trinity as a way of explaining relatedness, loving relationship**
Some regarded the idea of the Trinity as "useful language about social connectivity and loving relationships". One wrote: "It speaks to an underpinning 'relatedness' that applies throughout the universe. Every religion struggles with relatedness, even those religious perspectives that talk in terms of a net of connectedness. A net has both strings and holes, and relatedness between strings and holes is what makes the net. More traditional religions have God and supplicant (and some add in gurus and saints as well), or in Buddhism a Bodhisattva and a disciple. These are relations of two. But there is something I like very much about the old Hindu saying which points at a trinity: 'You think you understand two, because you understand one, where one and one makes two. But first you must understand 'and'.'"

## *Unitarian views about the Bible*

The Bible, which combines the Hebrew scriptures and the Christian New Testament, is the sacred text for Christians. Until fairly recently it was also much used in Unitarian worship and was the foundation on which the faith was based. But in recent decades, particularly in certain congregations and groups, it has fallen out of use. Respondents were offered the following options:

- It is the divinely inspired Word of God.
- It is a collection of books, written by humans over the centuries.
- It contains a mixture of history, mythology, poetry, wisdom, and good advice.
- It is but one of many sources of spiritual insight and wisdom.
- It is irrelevant to my Unitarian beliefs and worship.

Their choices are shown in Figure 7.4. By far the most popular combination of options was 'Collection of books, human authors' + 'Mixture of genres' + 'One of many sources of wisdom', which attracted 156 votes (61 per cent).

The other respondents chose different options, but only a small number opted for each combination. Comments on this question were very varied, and are summarised below.

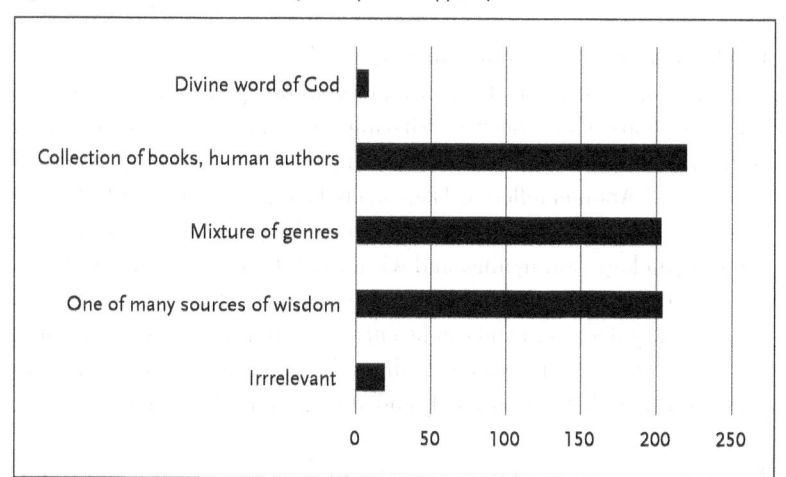

Figure 7.4: Views about the Bible (from options supplied)

| View | Count |
|---|---|
| Divine word of God | ~10 |
| Collection of books, human authors | ~220 |
| Mixture of genres | ~205 |
| One of many sources of wisdom | ~205 |
| Irrrelevant | ~20 |

### The Bible's role in Western culture and heritage

Several participants commented on the Bible as a foundation of Western culture. One wrote: "It is a fascinating example of human creativity and is the foundation of Western civilisation and culture. There are many non-religious reasons for studying it." Another called it "the most important source of spirituality in Western culture". Two others had contrasting views of its personal importance to them. One wrote: "It has impacted upon my thinking/ culture, but is not essential to my Unitarian thinking or belief." The other commented: "It's very important to me as part of my heritage. I love the language and the familiarity of certain passages. ... I know a lot of the stories and they continue to enrich my life – for instance, I appreciate references in literature, and certain phrases pop into my head when I am out walking."

### The Bible is a (not the) divinely inspired word of God
Some people reflected on the Bible as *a* (rather than *the*) divinely inspired Word of God. One wrote: "It *contains* the Word of God, not that it is the Word of God. It is authoritative for me, but there are other sources of spiritual wisdom which are valid for people of other faiths and those of no faith."

### The Bible as a conversation with God
A few respondents implied concurrence with one participant's statement that "The people who wrote it were having a conversation with their concept of the divine." One called it: "The early Judaeo-Christian interpretation of God's word". Another reflected: "Personally, I tend to find the Old Testament more relevant and more 'believable' than the New Testament. The former is the mythology, law, hymns, and wisdom of the Ancient Israelites that, among other things, reflects their dialectical relationship with god, though it has no singular vision and can be engaged with much as with any other literature. The New Testament is the writings of an esoteric end-times personality cult that has obviously ended up profoundly influential."

### The Bible as an important resource for understanding Christianity and Unitarianism
One person suggested that it is "unreliable, perhaps, but the major source for understanding Jesus, his teaching and the tradition out of which he emerged". Another wrote: "Sufficient knowledge of the Bible is necessary to understand Christianity and how it relates to the Unitarian position." One commented: "I use the Bible in worship and have spent my life studying it. ... But I have absolutely no belief in it as a direct revelation from God. ... In addition, I think we have misunderstood and misinterpreted the Bible with quite disastrous consequences. We Unitarians need to re-examine our attitudes to the Bible, and then perhaps we can reclaim it as a source of spiritual nurture."

### A critical approach is important
Some respondents warned that a critical approach is essential. One wrote: "It could be a source of spiritual insight and wisdom and contains some

good advice, but it has to be approached carefully. Too many things that can be easily misinterpreted and could possibly cause problems (e.g. anti-gay groups often quote the Bible)." Another suggested that it is "all down to the reading we give it". One reflected: "If it were newly discovered with none of its religious associations and baggage, it would be seen as one of the most important records of life as it was lived in the early days of recorded history." One person saw it as "a special book of spiritual wisdom", whereas another called it "A book of words ... not a manual for real-life living".

**The Bible also contains bad advice/unpalatable concepts**
Several respondents commented on Option 3 ('It contains a mixture of history, mythology, poetry, wisdom, and good advice') by adding "but also some bad advice!". One wrote: "It contains some unacceptable ideas, probably leading to much human suffering." Another agreed: "It also contains some descriptions of disasters and mass killings and torture and individual abuse that are the last word in cruelty and horror. ... It contains some bad advice." Some took issue with the Bible's depiction of the Divine. One person wrote: "It also contains some grossly wrong ideas about the Divine – e.g. that God is male, can be angry, and can feel vengeance." And finally another person considered that the Bible "does not reflect the inclusive ethos of Unitarianism. ... Our spiritual texts need to encompass society's diversity, so that everyone is regularly included, reflected, and represented."

## *Summary of findings*

It was noted in the first chapter that the vast majority of respondents (more than 85 per cent) came to Unitarianism as adults. The comments made in this chapter and the following ones show that many came to the movement from Christianity, bringing some of their beliefs and views with them. For example, although only a tiny minority still believe that Jesus was the unique Son of God, many of the others still find his teachings and example to be significant in their lives. Some believe that he was more than human, and that the more supernatural elements of Jesus' life and death were crucial to his message. Although, judging by the responses, the figure of Jesus is of varying significance to contemporary Unitarians, very few (19: 7 per cent) find him and his teachings irrelevant.

Respondents' attitudes to and beliefs about the [Holy] Spirit are somewhat more ambiguous. Nearly a quarter of them find the concept irrelevant, while the rest have some perception of God as Spirit as a presence in their lives. Fifty-six per cent see it as "The divine spark of God that dwells within each human being"; another 35 per cent as "The Divine breath that 'inspires' us with Life"; and nearly 30 per cent as "The 'Divine DNA" that is present in every living thing, not just human beings". Some used the term "Spirit" as a synonym for the Divine; some see it as a force working through human beings or from within them; while some see it as a personification of the Divine Feminine. It is clear from the foregoing that the [Holy] Spirit is an important part of many respondents' spiritual lives, but not necessarily in the Christian understanding of that term; while for others, it is not a relevant concept.

As Unitarianism came into existence as a reaction against the doctrine of the Trinity, it is perhaps unsurprising that many respondents reject the concept on doctrinal grounds. Yet for some it is a way of explaining relatedness, or loving relationship, while for others it is a useful way of approaching the mystery that is God.

The Bible, Christianity's sacred text, used to feature regularly in Unitarian worship services, but is now less often quoted. Participants' views about it vary widely. It is still of central importance to the faith of some; it is selectively approved by others, with the caveat that we must take a critical approach to reading it; but it is perceived as irrelevant by a few.

From the foregoing, it might be concluded that even though many respondents no longer describe themselves as Christians (although some certainly do), the central tenets and sacred text of Christianity are still significant to many, and play an important role in their faith and spiritual lives.

## *Questions for reflection and group discussion*

1. How important is the figure of Jesus to you as a Unitarian?
2. How would you describe the Holy Spirit? Is it relevant to your faith/spirituality?
3. What do you believe about the concept of the Trinity?

# Chapter 8
# Unitarians and Christian festivals

*In humble reverence and love*
*We celebrate the changing world;*
*Thankful and glad to live and move*
*As part of all that's new and old.*

Bruce Findlow, *Hymns for Living*, 31

This chapter will consider Unitarian attitudes to Christian festivals, and the impact that these have (or don't have) on the lives of Unitarians and on Unitarian worship. Respondents were asked: "Which Christian festivals/events, if any, are most significant for you?" Twenty-four people answered: "None", and a further 17 chose not to answer this question, which may be significant in itself. The following options were offered:

- Lent
- Easter
- Pentecost/Whitsuntide
- Harvest
- Advent/Christmas
- Other

The choices made by respondents are shown in Figure 8.1. Fifty-three people (21 per cent) did not choose any of the above festivals. Twenty-seven (11 per cent) chose Advent/ Christmas only; 19 (7 per cent) chose Harvest only; and 9 (3 per cent) chose Easter only. Some respondents chose more than one festival as having significance for them, these being the most popular combinations:

- 'Easter' + 'Harvest' + 'Advent/Christmas' (31: 12 per cent)
- 'Harvest' + 'Advent/Christmas' (29: 11 per cent)

Other respondents who answered this question found more meaning in different combinations of festivals; only a small number opted for each combination. The other Christian festivals mentioned included St. David's Day; All Saints; All Souls; Remembrance Sunday; Candlemas; Palm Sunday; Good Friday; and Trinity Sunday. Two people suggested that for them "ordinary Sundays are often more significant than festivals". Another commented: "None are especially significant to me any more. Every day is special. 'Everything is holy now'."

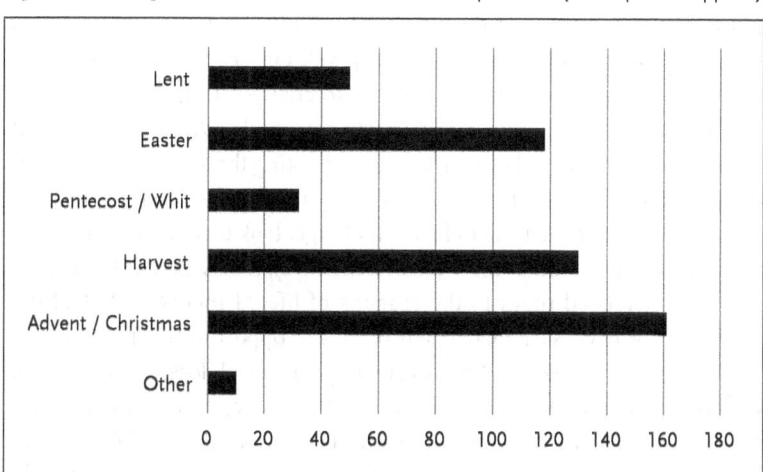

Figure 8.1: The Significance of Christian Festivals for Respondents (from options supplied)

One participant suggested: "Festivals are points for celebration and reflection so should include those of other faiths ... like Diwali, Samhain, Imbolc, Beltane, Lughnasadh, and Eid." Another wrote: "As someone who conducts worship, I find the above very useful as a platform from which to begin." Two people preferred the festivals of the Pagan Wheel of the Year. Another respondent ("very post-Christian") commented: "I tolerate these Christian festivals now, but things might change. I think you have to do them all or none. I don't mind them being referred to in an illustrative/ interest capacity."

Respondents were then asked a supplementary question: "Please explain why [these festivals are significant to you] in the text box below." Fifty-one people (20 per cent) did not answer this supplementary question. Some made general comments, while others made comments on specific festivals, which will be covered later.

## *General comments*

### Marking the seasons of the year

Many respondents found these festivals significant because they "mark turning points in the seasons of the year". One commented that their value was "as seasonal rites that relate to changes in nature, ourselves, give us insight, hope, solace and practices/ rituals". Another suggested: "It is important to have landmark events denoting the seasons/ changes in the year (e.g. abundant food, remembering those worse off), the longest/ shortest day, and have time to focus, recharge, look forward/look back etc. If we can use these traditional 'tools' in this way, then where is the harm?"

Another related them to the seasons of life: "I increasingly feel that festivals, not necessarily Christian ones, are opportunities to focus in a powerful way on seasons of the world, hope, renewal, loss, our interaction with consuming Earth's resources. Festivals are an opportunity to have fun and engage with others, as well as to reflect on serious themes." One person liked festivals for the music, writing: "Christian festivals mark the regular ritual of the year. For me they have lost any religious significance, but I do appreciate the great Festival Masses and other oratorios and sacred music."

### Part of our culture, tradition, and upbringing

Some participants believed that the significance of the traditional festivals comes from the fact that we "live in a Christian country – however nominal", but believed that these days "Christmas and Easter have a secular significance but not a religious one". One respondent explained: "I celebrate a secular Christmas, inspired by the morality of Dickens' *A Christmas Carol*, Pratchett's *Hogfather*, and belief in the magic of childhood. I acknowledge the Christian elements of this festival, and am very fond of the music." Others stated that the significance of these festivals was more about tradition and upbringing. One commented: "Festivals are part of our common heritage, binding us together and comforting us, yet also challenging us."

### Why Christian festivals are meaningful and relevant

There was a variety of reasons why Christian festivals were meaningful and relevant to some respondents. For some it was an opportunity to "connect us to those who have been before and to do something larger than us all. It feels special to honour sacred days and feel a connection to our Christian roots." For others, the roots of Unitarianism in Christianity provided the reason: "They are the essential Christian festivals on which our faith is based."

Some mentioned particular enjoyable elements: "great hymns, readings and celebrations, and time for thought". Another suggested that they give us things to celebrate, and "If taken allegorically, they are opportunities for spiritual reflection". Others saw them as "an opportunity for bonding communities round a commonly understood focal point from our culture, which has included the Christian story for centuries". Some suggested that "rituals connect humans through the ages"; that they "bring people together in community"; that they are "great opportunities for sharing"; that they have "symbolic significance". One person commented: "All these festivals have relevance and lessons to teach us on an everyday level, as do the Celtic festivals of the Wheel of the Year. "

## Why Christian festivals are not meaningful or relevant
A number of respondents commented on the reasons why they do not find these Christian festivals significant. One wrote: "No Christian festivals are significant to me because all the Christian festivals ... developed from a Trinitarian theology." Others explained that they identified themselves as humanist or post-Christian, so the festivals were no longer relevant to them. One suggested: "We need a new set of festivals and faith seasons."

## Other faiths' festivals more meaningful or relevant
Several participants pointed out that some of the Christian festivals have either Pagan roots or Pagan elements, particularly Easter, Harvest, and Christmas. One explained: "Celebrating the equinoxes and solstices makes more sense to me, as I can relate my life to the changing seasons. To me, the Jesus story is a metaphor for the sun's journey throughout the year as it appears to die and rise again." Another commented:

> *I follow the Pagan wheel of the year or eightfold festivals, and the Christian liturgical calendar dovetails rather nicely into these, for me. I value Lent as a time of deeper contemplations and evaluation of my spiritual path for the year, Easter as a celebration of new life in the springtime, Harvest as a time of gratitude for the Earth's abundance, and Advent/ Christmas as a time to deepen into the darkness and focus on inner work, while anticipating the return of the light at the rebirth of the sun.*

One person commented that "although happy to attend Christian events to celebrate family and friendship, [I] find more resonance with festivals from other faiths, as well as festivals from the secular/ humanist tradition if they celebrate values I share. The festivals/ events that most resonate with me ... are Diwali, Holi, Eid al Adha, Eid al Fitr, summer and winter solstices, Songkran."

## *The significance of Lent*

Respondents had a variety of reasons for marking Lent.

**A time for self-examination**
For some, "It is an annual opportunity to do some self-examination, and to try to change for the better". Another commented: "My early Anglican upbringing taught me that self-discipline is a good thing, so I practise some form at the appropriate time." One person explained: "Lent has become part of my latter-day spiritual practice: a time for reflection, renewal." Another commented: "Lent and Holy Week: connection and clearing out, shouldering of responsibility for suffering, meditation and asceticism, spiritual fitness."

**A time to give something up**
Others associated Lent more with giving something up. One wrote: "Lent supports fasting or giving up something in a way that many other religions do, and this is a reminder about how generally lucky we are. It focuses the mind." Another explained: "I choose to observe Lent by choosing not to spend money on things I don't need, just essentials and give money to a charity." One commented that they had "given up things for Lent for non-religious reasons", while another believed that "The self-sacrifice of Lent is relevant even without belief in God".

## *The significance of Easter*

Fifty-three respondents (21 per cent) commented on the significance of Easter for them. They ranged from those who believed it to be "The most vital event in the Christian calendar" through to those who saw it as an important Spring festival, and those who enjoyed the secular aspects of it.

## Easter as a Christian festival

Two people who believe in its high Christian significance described it as follows: "Easter – the Paschal Mystery – LIFE – DEATH – RESURRECTION – our story"; and "God the Perennial, renewed and renewing, The Source, The insistent Beyond and Other, The Incomprehensible, The Life, The All".

For one, it marked "The farewell to a loving genius of his time under cruel circumstances". Another commented: "There is sadness ... at Easter. I never fail to be emotionally affected by Jesus' crucifixion, along with many past and ongoing instances of 'man's cruelty to man'." Another stated: "Easter, because it is about the refusal of a good man to recant in order to save his life. So Good Friday is the only day of relevance."

For others, Easter was a time of "reflection on the cost of doing good for others but good prevailing over evil with the resurrection story". One wrote: "Easter symbolises rebirth and renewal as the necessary consequence of the continuity of life, and also the ultimate triumph of good over evil." In the minds of some respondents, it celebrated "new life and ways in which resurrection can occur in human lives" and the prospect that "Death is a new beginning". One wrote: "Even Easter can have a symbolic meaning for Unitarians. You cannot kill what is truly loving." Another commented: "Whilst a literal resurrection is problematic to me, the idea of rebirth is not, particularly in spring, so I see this as actually quite a good inter-faith theme."

For some participants, it was about remembering Jesus; as one wrote: "because Jesus was a brave and remarkable man who gave his life and has influenced people down the centuries and will continue to do so in centuries to come, so he should be remembered with the utmost respect and love". Several mentioned that for them Easter was a time of "new beginnings and new hope". One commented: "Easter represents rebirth and the eternal message of hope. I believe that the resurrection is metaphorical rather than corporeal." For another, it was "a reminder of the cyclical nature of all things".

## Easter as a Spring festival

For many respondents, Easter was more related to Springtime and new life than it was to the death and purported resurrection of Jesus. One saw it as a "lunar festival of rebirth, rather than Christian". Several saw it as "a joyous celebration of life and Spring, a reawakening"; another regarded it as "symbolic of the renewal of life in Spring, after the 'death' of Winter. The increasing length of daylight hours is restorative to me after a dark season." Some people mentioned the Pagan links with or antecedents of Easter. One commented that Easter and Harvest had significance for them "Because they coincide with the Celtic festivals and have meaning for me". Of course some Unitarians may see Easter both as a significant festival about Jesus and also as related to Springtime and new life.

**Easter as a secular festival**
One person commented on their enjoyment of the more secular aspects of Easter, saying: "We have a 30-year tradition of egg rolling and an outdoor picnic with friends, so it's a special time. I like to make an Easter decoration with blossom, decorated eggs etc as a centrepiece to bring spring into the house."

## The significance of Pentecost/Whitsuntide

Only a few respondents commented on the significance of Pentecost or Whit. Two people mentioned that it "marks the birth of the Christian church".

**The tradition of Whit Walks**
Some mentioned the English tradition of Whit Walks. One recalled: "Whit used to be significant to me as a child, as all the members of my church and all the members of all other churches (except the Catholics) walked together through the town with banners and flowers and bands. Then in the afternoon we had a picnic in a local park. It was about bearing witness. Now that other religious groups ... are confident enough to walk to celebrate, then I think we should think about recreating the Whit Walks and possibly making them multi-faith."

### The link to the Spirit
But the most frequently cited reason for finding significance in Pentecost was its link to the Spirit. One respondent wrote: "I like to mark Pentecost as a reminder of the possibility of human beings being open to divine inspiration." Another called it "a celebration of the Spirit". Finally, one person commented: "Pentecost – I think being able to speak and be understood by all is a great image (and perhaps one that Unitarians ought to make a bit more of)."

## *The significance of Harvest*

Harvest is a festival much loved by Unitarians. Respondents saw it as an opportunity to give thanks and express their gratitude for the bounty of the earth, and to care for others. For some, it was a time to appreciate the beauties of the natural world. One wrote: "Harvest is part of the Christian tradition, but also fits my leanings towards celebrating nature."

### A time of gratitude and thanksgiving
The theme of gratitude was a common one. One person wrote: "We all need food, and it is good to remember all those who work to provide it for us and to remember to cherish our world and the seasons." Another saw it as "symbolic of the manifestation of all that is good in the world, not only the ripened crops and fruit, but also the good in human beings". One commented: "Harvest makes me realise what a fantastic world we live in – and if there is a God, then we need to say thank you to him."

### A reminder to care for the earth and each other
Some saw it as "a reminder to take care of the earth". One suggested that it was about "how humans interact with the environment and share our resources". Another reflected: "I think modern life is no less precarious than when we had to worry about whether a harvest would succeed or fail. Hence I think Harvest time fulfils a need to manage a very primal set of anxieties that I share with most people. It also prompts me to remember the Food Bank Collection which I am glad my church participates in."

### A metaphor for in-gathering and reflection

One saw Harvest as "a metaphor for in-gathering and reflection". This was put more poetically by another, who commented: "Harvest: God is that which knows how to grow. God of consolidation and putting into mindful practice, God of maturing and seasoning, God also of loitering and noon-day slumber. Fruiting and harvesting, shrivelling and withdrawing, closing in and shutting down. Nurturing the soul in the growing dark, until advent comes again with its expectation."

### Harvest not really a Christian festival

Some respondents commented that Harvest was not really a Christian festival. One wrote: "I have chosen Harvest because it is the least 'Christian'. ... It is the time when I give thanks for the joys of Spring and Summer, and prepare my mind for the coming Autumn and Winter." Another shared a Pagan understanding of it: "Lammas as a festival of gratitude. Also lunar, from Old English *haerfest* (Autumn) and held at the Harvest Moon." A third wrote simply: "Harvest is the only one which has relevance for me, and this is because it is a seasonal, earth-based celebration of earth's bounty."

## *The significance of Advent*

Although the festivals of Advent and Christmas were combined in the original question, several respondents made specific comments about the significance of Advent in their supplementary answers.

### A time of anticipation and expectation

Some saw Advent as a time of "joyous anticipation", of "expectation and joy". One connected it "with the idea of waiting with bated breath at the darkest part of the year for the magical epiphany of light, life and hope". Another reported: "During Advent for the past few years each day I've read a chapter of a book called *The Christmas Mystery* by Jostein Gaarder. ... It tells the 'Christmas Story' in a different way, as a journey backwards through time and space."

### A time for quiet reflection

Other people used Advent as "a time for withdrawing into myself for the winter season, and the coming of a more reflective season". One called it a "time of quiet and being inwardly reflective, while at the same time being open to the dawning of new light". Another saw it as "a time to deepen into the darkness and focus on inner work, while anticipating the return of the light at the rebirth of the sun". One person described a personal practice during Advent: "It is a time to work through darkness to light, to experience each week peace, joy, hope and love with candles, and use the time to once again examine ourselves. ... It is a waiting, preparation time to be used *slowly*, not in the rush that is usually Christmas."

## *The significance of Christmas*

A large number of respondents (86: 33 per cent) made comments about Christmas, most of which were positive.

### A cultural Christian festival

Some just liked it "because it's Christmas". One commented: "The tale of Christmas has been absorbed into the British culture, and most people celebrate with their families and friends, which is helpful if not overdone." Another wrote: "If we implemented the Christian message – good will to all – the world would be a better place."

### The celebration of Jesus' birth

This was a typical comment: "Happy to celebrate the birth of Jesus of Nazareth and the idea of loving kindness as a goal of living". Others saw it as "a time of joy and hope" or "a time of peace and love, not just for Unitarians/ Christians, but for all". One reflected that "Although it is 'mythic' (both in the technical sense, and because it may not be 'historical'), it celebrates the incarnation in Jesus and in all of us." Another suggested: "It is the time when humans recognised that God was part of our humanity in the form of a baby. Humans recognised a God within themselves through the life of Jesus and his recorded teachings. God became one with us; of creation, recreation, co-creation, essence, evolution and eternity."

Two people commented on the modern symbolism of the Christmas story. One explained: "There are great themes we can all connect with and use, as they are absolutely relevant today around refugees (the flight into Egypt, even though I don't believe it actually happened); homelessness (no room at the inn); poverty; the world turned upside down (the Magnificat); good news to the poor."

## A time for sharing with family and friends

For many respondents, the most important aspect of Christmas was getting together with family and friends. One wrote simply: "I love Christmas, a time to celebrate lots of love with family and friends, a time to sing and light candles." Another commented: "It is important for me personally because it refocuses our thinking on the family and all that can mean ... for myself and others – a real emphasis on community." This was linked in many people's minds to the "meaning of the season". One wrote: "Christmas to me is about family and being thankful for the loving connections we have in our lives." Another admitted: "I enjoy Christmas purely for the sentiment of good-will and the uplift in everyone's mood. I see no relevance to any religious or spiritual belief, although I respect others who do."

## A mid-Winter festival

Some participants appreciated Christmas at least partly as a mid-Winter festival. One wrote: "Christmas is much needed in December – longest night, shortest day of the year, people tend to be depressed due to weather so we need that joyful celebration, and I let myself be carried away by the magic and myths around Christmas." Another described it as "That mid-winter time when we get together with friends and family, we remind ourselves that Spring will come, the darkness of winter will end, that we have other human beings for company and comfort". Some saw it as a time for "closing down, resting, reflection", to look back over the past year, and forward to the next one.

### Problems with Christmas

Christmas was not seen as a positive, joyous time by all respondents. One wrote simply: "Christmas I have avoided for years." Another called it "a family event and a chance to celebrate", but reflected that "because of that, those without family can find it hard. It raises issues also about excess, expenditure, and expectations." It was described by another person as "ruined by feasting and commercialism". Another struggled with it, commenting: "I feel very hypocritical at Christmas; I am not good with mangers and stars leading wise men. The pagan is dominant, and I tend to rejoice more in the coming of longer days and warmth. I find most Christmas carols very difficult to sing when my mind rejects so much of the content. I appreciate Christmas cards, so many sent with love…"

## *The significance of other Christian festivals*

Some respondents mentioned other Christian festivals that they personally found significant. Palm Sunday was mentioned without specific comment. Other days that were valued by some people were All Saints: "a respect for those who have lived exemplary lives"; All Souls, "because people need a space to reflect on death/ mortality and to remember those who've passed on"; Candlemas, "beginning the increasing of light"; and Saint David's Day, "because all over Wales there is poetry and music and celebration in the ancient Welsh language".

## *Summary of findings*

Apart perhaps from the Flower Communion service, Unitarians do not have any festivals of their own. The principal Christian festivals are widely celebrated or marked by Unitarian congregations in the United Kingdom, and are still significant for many respondents. Lent, Easter, Pentecost/ Whit, Harvest, Advent, and Christmas all have support to varying degrees. Some people find them a useful way of marking the seasons of the year;

some believe that they are an important part of their culture, tradition, and upbringing; some enjoy the specifically Christian elements of them, while others have different interpretations.

Lent has spiritual significance for some respondents, as an opportunity for self-examination and self-discipline, and as an opportunity for spiritual reflection. The significance of Easter ranges from the traditional Christian message, through to its importance as a Spring festival, and to a more secular appreciation. Pentecost/ Whit is most often seen in terms of celebrating humankind's link to the Spirit, while the primary meanings of Harvest for respondents are about gratitude for the bounty of the earth, an appreciation of the beauties of the natural world, and a reminder to take care of the Earth and other people. Advent is seen as either a time of anticipation and expectation or as an opportunity for quiet reflection.

Respondents have many views on Christmas. Some see it as a cultural Christian festival – the celebration of the birth of Jesus; some enjoy it as a time for sharing with family and friends; while others find its significance as a mid-Winter festival. Some see it as a secular celebration at a dark time of year. Some believe that it has become over-commercialised; but for most participants, Christmas is perceived as a joyful festival, with varying degrees of religious significance.

Other festivals were mentioned by some people as being significant to them personally, while others enjoy "ordinary Sundays" just as much. Overall, it is clear that Christian festivals still play a role in the lives of respondents, and perhaps in the lives of most Unitarians in Britain today. Some celebrate them as other Christians do; some find other reasons to celebrate them.

## *Question for reflection and group discussion*

1. *Which Christian festivals, if any, are signficant for you? Why?*

# Chapter 9
# Unitarians' relationship with other faith traditions

*Whatever name, whatever faith,*
*At heart we share a common bond,*
*A shared humanity in God,*
*Whose name and character is love.*

Andrew Pratt, Sing Your Faith, 155

The sixth section of the survey investigated respondents' relationships with other faith traditions. Respondents were asked: "Is there another faith tradition which is important in your life? Please name it/them below." They were given the following options, and invited to choose all that were relevant to them:

- Mainstream Christianity
- Paganism
- Hinduism
- Bahá-i Faith
- Sikhism
- Islam
- Buddhism
- Judaism
- Taoism
- Sunday Assembly ('atheist church')
- Other
- None of the above.

Their choices are shown in Figure 9.1. Three faith traditions attracted a number of votes on their own: 'Mainstream Christianity': 36 (14 per cent); 'Buddhism': 18 (7 per cent); and Paganism: 15 (5 per cent). Fifty-three respondents (21 per cent) ticked 'Mainstream Christianity' and a combination of other option(s). If one includes the first four categories named below, which are aspects of Christianity judged by respondents to be 'outside' the mainstream, the total number influenced by some form of Christianity goes up to 109 (42 per cent).

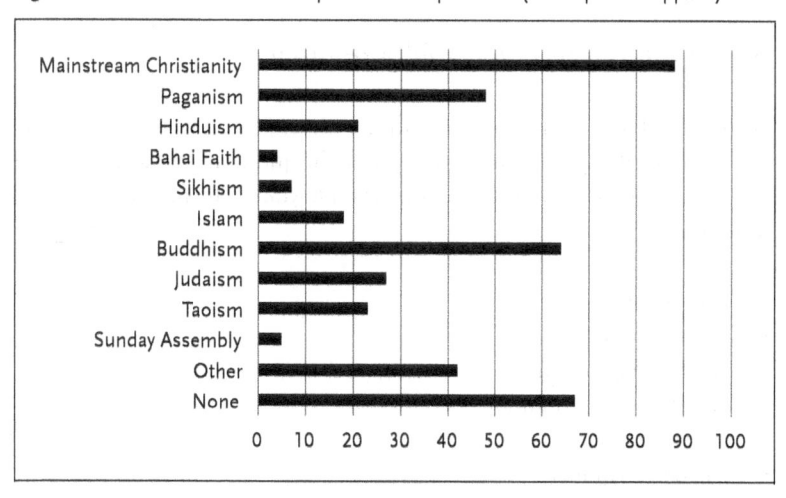

Figure 9.1: Other Faith Traditions important to Respondents (from options supplied)

It may also be deduced, perhaps, that for a significant proportion of respondents (the 67 who ticked 'None of the above' and the eight who did not answer this question: 29 per cent in total), Unitarianism suffices. As always, the 'Other' box attracted a fair number of responses, including the following popular choices:

- Liberal Christianity/Liberal Catholicism/Anabaptism
- Mystics/Contemplative Christianity
- Celtic/Findhorn Christianity

- Religious Society of Friends (Quakers)
- Sufism

Other faith traditions such as Reform Judaism and Native American spirituality were referenced by a few individuals, as were non-faith influences such as Science. More general comments such as "All of the above are worthy of time and respect" and "I live in a largely (but not exclusively) Christian culture and in a multi-faith world" suggest a broad interest in other faiths.

## *Important aspects of these faith traditions*

Having established which other faith traditions (if any) were important to respondents, the questionnaire next posed the question: "What aspect(s) of this/ these faith traditions is/are important to you?" The following options were offered:

- The rituals
- The sacred texts
- The beliefs/doctrines
- The stories and traditions
- The devotional practices
- The ethics/morals.

The respondents' choices are shown in Figure 9.2. Sixty people (23 per cent) did not answer this question, representing most of those who had answered "none" to the previous question. Sixteen (6 per cent) chose all six aspects. Of all the aspects, 'Ethics and morals' was the most popular. Thirteen (5 per cent) ticked this option only, and a further 49 (19 per cent) chose this option and a combination of others. Many people also chose to comment on particular aspects of the faith traditions that they had identified in the previous question. Some of these comments are shared below.

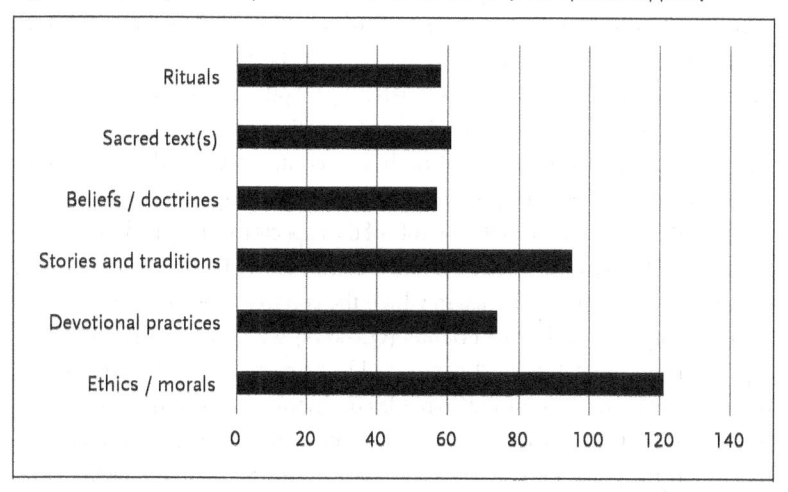

Figure 9.2: The important aspects of other Faith Traditions (from options supplied)

[Bar chart showing approximate values:
- Rituals: ~60
- Sacred text(s): ~62
- Beliefs / doctrines: ~58
- Stories and traditions: ~95
- Devotional practices: ~75
- Ethics / morals: ~122]

The relationship with other faiths attracted comment: "There are elements in most of these traditions which speak to me, illuminate my thinking and warm my heart. But there's nothing here that I would accept uncritically"; and "I wouldn't go so far as to say 'important in my life', but some of the principles and writings of the above enrich my view on life."

For some, the inter-faith aspect was important, and they were actively involved with multi-faith groups in their communities. One wrote: "I like to explore the common ground between faith traditions and find what seems relevant to me from different sources." Another commented: "It is important to understand our roots and to learn about the faith traditions of our neighbours."

**Mainstream Christianity** attracted the largest number of comments. Nine people commented that they had been brought up in the Christian faith, and still valued it. One explained: "It is the most familiar, the faith I know the most about from childhood, not because it is necessarily better or more complete than other faiths, nor because I 'believe' in it more than other teachings. It is simply more part of my culture." Others wrote of its importance "in shaping my life and faith up to today" or of "a sense of connection to my religious heritage which I cannot completely abandon".

Three mentioned the importance of the teachings of Jesus. One wrote: "While I do not literally believe much of the Bible, I do try to adhere to the teachings of Jesus, as I believe they are the best on offer!" One person asserted: "Liberal non-Unitarian Christianity inspires me and challenges me – removing me from my comfort zone." Another commented: "Christian writers, theologians, history and traditions continue to yield insights into my personal faith." Two respondents mentioned the importance of Christian devotional practices, and another wrote of the aspects that they had valued as a member of different Christian churches: communion, the social aspects, and the various different ministries in which the congregations were involved.

**The Religious Society of Friends (Quakers)** was generally perceived as separate from mainstream Christianity. Eleven participants cited it as being important to them, and some also made comments. One noted its "similarity in many ways to Unitarianism". Another commented: "For me the Quaker meeting is the perfect way of communing with my Sense of the Divine. The descending of the silence holds a very special essence for me, and, although I enjoy Unitarian services, the gathering to sit and just be seems wonderful. I feel closer to the Divine in this form of meeting than any other service."

**Buddhism** was also mentioned quite frequently. Two respondents cited "the Buddha's emphasis on compassion for all beings". Others appreciated the "very practically useful wisdom, ideas and practices" of this tradition. One suggested that it is "more receptive and reflective than our Western Christian tradition. I think we can learn from that." Another commented: "Meditation is a valuable tool for life and for the spiritual life. Some of the Buddhist teachings (do no harm, avoid attachment) are appealing. I find the life story of Gautama just as moving as that of Jesus." Several people commented about the Buddhist devotional practices which they had incorporated into their spiritual lives, such as the person who wrote: "Buddhist meditation practices are an important part of my spiritual life, and I have found Buddhist retreats to be very helpful."

Some respondents favoured the approach of **Hinduism**. One wrote: "Hindu teaching helps me to see God in everything." Another valued the Hindu concept of *ahimsa*, or non-violence, which is also taught by Buddhism and Jainism. A third commented on the practical "how to live teachings", and two others mentioned the Hindu belief in reincarnation as being important to them.

The other Eastern religion mentioned in the comments was **Taoism.** One person commented: "I love the *Tao Te Ching*, and the underlying ethics and morals contained in it." Another appreciated "the concept of both masculine and feminine divine" which Taoism shares with Paganism. A third wrote: "Taoist moral teaching makes me laugh (a rare quality in most religious scriptures)."

**Paganism** was attractive to some participants. One suggested that it "is also an important part of British heritage, as these festivals pre-date Christianity". Others enjoyed its "relish of the senses and the material aspects of creation". One valued "The exploration of the world and all that makes up the world as one divine entirety and how the world's rhythms and patterns are joined". Two commented on "The idea of the wheel of the year: change, renewal, life and death, a way of passionately expressing the profundity of life". Other features singled out for comment included Paganism's respect for the natural world; its philosophy of acceptance; and the 'no harm' rule. One respondent particularly appreciated Paganism's "insistence on the Divine Feminine, and on the overt inclusion of non-heterosexual, non-cis gender divinities. ... It's very refreshing for a LGBTQIA alphabet-soup person to see beings like myself actively represented in a pantheon, rather than denied existence or lumped together with everyone else."

Five participants had mentioned **Sufism**, the mystical branch of Islam, in answer to the previous question. Two of them mentioned the importance to them of the "devotional poetry of the ... Sufi mystics Rumi and Hafiz". Two others mentioned the value of **mysticism** "in all traditions". One commented: "some of my favourite spiritual teachers and writers are from other traditions e.g. Rumi, John O'Donohue, Rabindranath Tagore, Lao Tse." Another was "fascinated by the way that the thoughts of the Mystics and a lot of modern scientists can be seen as converging".

Other respondents appreciated the "oneness of all humanity espoused by the Bahá-i Faith"; the "family values" of Judaism; and the behavioural sciences, which one respondent suggested "contain modern forms of most of the wisdom in the ancient texts".

## How these faith traditions 'sit' within the Unitarian faith

The final question in this section of the survey asked respondents "How does it/do they sit within your Unitarian faith?" Although 84 people (33 per cent) did not answer this question, the responses of the rest reflected the many influences of other faith traditions on contemporary Unitarians. They are summarised in the shared comments below.

### Comfortably/compatibly (or not)

Many participants commented that their other faith affiliations sat comfortably within or alongside their Unitarianism, or were compatible with it. One went so far as to write: "For me they are inseparable ... my Unitarianism and Pagan/Buddhist beliefs and practices are intertwined." A few had reservations. One included the caveat "where they coincide with my reason and conscience". Another commented: "There are some aspects of other faiths that do not sit so well with my Unitarian faith or are difficult to accept: original sin, atonement, religion being sealed; some rules might seem unnecessary or strange to me, also the role of women in other faiths."

### The inclusivity of Unitarianism

Some respondents commented on the inclusive approach of Unitarianism. One wrote: "My Unitarian faith encompasses all those faiths." Another wrote simply: "As a broad-church Unitarian I believe we are all free to find our own spiritual path." One commented: "They advise and inform my practice and my contemplation. They act as counterpoints when I have got too much absorbed into one perspective. They help me understand the perspectives of others within my congregation and the wider British public." Another wondered: "Is Unitarianism a faith? It is so wide in its acceptance of contradictory beliefs." But this breadth and tolerance was valued by another, who commented: "They are what brought me to Unitarianism, as a religious tradition and company in which I could learn and grow with fellow seekers."

### Other faiths enriching Unitarian faith, or completely separate?

Many participants commented that other faith traditions enrich their Unitarian faith. One wrote: "I don't care what tradition some rituals or stories come from. If they carry a blessing, good word, good advice – I take them. I do however approach some of them with a healthy dose of rationalism." Another commented: "All religious understanding, from wherever it may be gleaned, sits comfortably within my Unitarian faith, whether it be to broaden a growing experience and understanding, or as a challenge to refine what remains as a coherent faith." A few saw their interaction with other faith traditions as "a separate compartment of my life". One person wrote: "They provide a knowledge disjuncture and option for me to choose to learn. They don't 'sit' within my Unitarian faith as such."

### How Unitarians relate to Christianity

For some respondents, their Christian roots blended happily with their Unitarian faith. One reflected: "I take my moral and ethical values from Unitarianism; however, I sometimes find a level of comfort and security in some of the rituals and traditions of other Christian denominations." Some commented on the relevance and importance of Christian devotional practices for their Unitarian faith. One commented: "I do not consider myself a Christian in the traditional sense, but value the Christian heritage of Unitarianism. I think that the teachings and life of Jesus are inspirational. ... The Christian teachings are probably still the most important to me at the moment, but mainly because they are the most familiar."

Others perceived Christianity as their "main dialogue partner". One wrote: "I see myself as firmly rooted in the Judaeo-Christian tradition, but am Universalist in my belief that all traditions have their merit, and can enhance/ expand my understanding of the divine." Another wrote of Christian teachings: "I can view them from an outsider standpoint as a Unitarian, while experiencing them from the insider standpoint of a Christian. I feel a flow between my Christianity and my Unitarianism." Another warned: "As Unitarians, we have to be careful that we don't belittle other faiths or assume that by moving from one tradition to another a person is rejecting their past religious journey. I still draw a lot from my Methodist journey, in which I learned the central importance of hospitality, and the importance of sharing stories."

### How Unitarians relate to the Religious Society of Friends

Respondents found the Religious Society of Friends (Quakers) very compatible with Unitarianism. One commented: "I do not find any problem or conflict with Quaker meeting and my Unitarian faith/practice. I have always been made to feel welcome at Quaker meeting and often find that Friends are interested to find out about my Unitarian beliefs." Another agreed: "I have a great respect for Friends and their views and attitudes. ... I might have gone down the Quaker path if I hadn't found the Unitarian one. And I think Friends and Unitarians have much in common."

### How Unitarians relate to Buddhism

Most of the people who commented on how Buddhism sits within their Unitarian faith wrote about the importance of Buddhist meditation and mindfulness practices, which they used in their daily lives. Others appreciated the philosophy, ethics, and precepts behind it. One commented: "Like Unitarianism, it promotes the idea of discovering your own truth in a non-doctrinal way, taking what you find useful and leaving that which you don't. It also promotes tolerance, compassion, and loving kindness to self and others." Another valued "the rigorous analysis of existence and suffering in Buddhism, along with the views about karma and the afterlife".

### How Unitarians relate to Paganism

Most of the participants who identified as Pagan stated that their Paganism sat comfortably with their Unitarian faith. One person commented: "I seem to have always been Pagan before I knew what the word meant, and I find I can comfortably run this alongside the moral code of Christianity and the freedom/ reason/ tolerance of a Unitarian approach." Another wrote: "It sits well as it is all about respect and care for ourselves, our planet and the people on it."

## How Unitarians relate to Hinduism
Three respondents commented about Hinduism. One wrote: "To me, God is the environment/ atmosphere/ energy etc. I think the Hindus see God in everything too." Another explained: "Both are aspects of my spiritual life – my relationship with, and service to, the Divine. Of all your questions, this is the hardest for me to answer, because it doesn't 'sit' within my Unitarian faith – yet they are fully compatible, for me, with each other."

## How Unitarians relate to Taoism
For one person, "Taoism has helped me form my beliefs, where Christian teaching didn't make sense." Another attended a Tao meditation and discussion group once a week, which is "very open and participative". A third enjoyed the fact that Taoism challenged "Unitarian rationalism and seriousness".

## How Unitarians relate to Judaism
Jewish respondents were happy with how their faith sits with Unitarianism. One commented: "I'm Jewish by birth as well as being a Unitarian. ... My Jewishness is important to me. And the virtues spelled out by the prophets and practices in the Hebrew Bible: concern for the poor, jubilee when debts are cancelled, the bar against charging interest on loans, the concern for refugees and foreigners and the Golden Rule ... seem absolutely congruent with Unitarian values. Plus, the idea of one God started (I believe) with the Jews. I see no contradiction between being Jewish and being Unitarian."

## How Unitarians relate to Islam
Two people believed it was important to "make some connection with Muslim neighbours". One wrote: "I have neighbours who are devout Muslims whom I respect and admire for their dedication to their chosen path." Another commented: "I respect other faiths, but Christianity and Islam, together with Judaism, are those which have had a significant effect on my outlook. Much of my thinking springs from my awareness of Muslim thinking and the unlikelihood that it's going to change any time soon."

## Summary of findings

The first question in this section asked respondents "Is there another faith tradition which is important in your life?" For a significant number of respondents (the 67 who ticked 'None of the above', and the eight who did not answer this question), it might be deduced that 'Unitarian' suffices. The analysis of the options in Figure 9.1 at the head of the chapter shows that 'Mainstream Christianity' is in numerical terms the primary 'other faith tradition' which is influential for respondents. While numbers may be smaller for other faiths, the respondents' comments throughout illustrate the considerable significance attached by some people to the values and practices of other faiths.

The other two questions in this section asked which aspects of these traditions were most important to participants, and how they fitted with their Unitarian faith. From the replies it may be concluded that many respondents have a rich and varied relationship with other faith traditions. Some traditions influence particular individuals more than others, most notably Mainstream Christianity, the Religious Society of Friends, Paganism, and Buddhism. These seem to fit most comfortably with their Unitarian faith. Most have a broad respect and tolerance for the beliefs and ethics of other faith traditions and have benefitted from incorporating devotional practices from other faiths into their spiritual lives. These responses demonstrate that Unitarians, while committed to questioning and critical appraisal, are open to the exploration of new ideas, new practices, and new ways of thinking.

## Questions for reflection and group discussion

1. Is there another faith tradition which is important to you? Why?
2. What aspects of other faith traditions do you find relevant to your Unitarian journey?
3. If you are active within another faith tradition, or use (for example) devotional practices from another faith tradition, how well does this sit within your Unitarian faith?

# Chapter 10
# *Unitarian views on evil, sin, and personal salvation*

> *I sent my soul some truth to win;*
> *My soul returned these words to tell:*
> *'Look not beyond, but turn within,*
> *For I myself am heaven and hell'.*

John Andrew Storey, *Hymns for Living*, 37

In this section of the survey, respondents were asked for their views on certain theological or spiritual concepts; text boxes were provided in which to share their responses. Their answers will be considered in this chapter and the next. This chapter will cover the concepts of 'the nature of evil', 'sin', and 'personal salvation'.

## Unitarians' views on the nature of evil

The question was "What do you believe about the nature of evil?" Reflections on this are divided into eight broad areas, as summarised in the shared comments below.

### 'Evil' is not a helpful term

Several participants struggled with the word 'evil' itself. One commented:

> *The main issues/questions asked by philosophers on the topic of evil have been: should we use the term 'evil' in our moral, political, and legal discourse and thinking, or is evil an out-dated or empty concept which*

*should be abandoned? What is the relationship between evil and other moral concepts such as badness and wrongdoing? I personally believe that the word is open to so many interpretations that it is not a helpful term.*

Others suggested that its use depends on one's personal perspective. This example was given: "When our soldiers fight, we think of them as heroic warriors against evil. [The other side's] soldiers are at best the unwitting servants of evil. I was ... married to an Austrian woman whose father was in the German army in WWII. He and my father were fighting on opposite sides. I just don't think that explaining what was happening in terms of evil is adequate." Another person thought that "it can be a lazy term to apply to humans or events that we do not understand".

## Distinction between 'natural' disasters and 'human-made' disasters

A few people made a distinction between natural disasters and human-made ones. One commented: "People talk of 'natural evils' like natural disasters, but that doesn't really fit the description of evil that I always think of. There are awful things that cause great harm which just happen due to the unfolding of the physical processes which govern the universe. For me, this does not count as 'evil', as there is no conscious intent (or even negligence) behind it." Another agreed, writing: "Natural evil is a consequence of the structure of the world. Human evil is a result of people's inability to empathise with others."

## 'Evil' as a human concept used to control others

Some respondents believed that evil is a "human-made concept, used to explain phenomena not easily understood in past times; an idea used to have power over others". Examples given included "how society is getting more selfish and self-obsessed"; "terrorist bombers"; "certain individuals such as psychopaths and sociopaths [who] have lost touch with their 'divine' nature"; and "newspaper editors who stir up religious/ racial/ class hatred".

## 'Evil' a separate active force in the world (or not)

Opinion was divided on whether evil is, or is not, a separate active force in the world. "Evil is not a specific 'thing/ devil' etc outside of human construction," articulated one side of the argument; on the other side, one person explained: "'Good' and 'evil' is (like light and dark) one of the basic dualities of creation, an aspect of the design of the world by [the Creator]. As human beings, we are frequently presented with choices between good and evil, or anyway between somewhat more good and less good, or rather more harmful and rather less so. 'Good' is what in the long run yields the fruits of greater happiness, bliss, peace, contentment, harmony, connection. 'Evil' is what separates us from or hampers our experiencing those satisfying and delightful feelings."

## Evil as a turning away from good/God

Others saw evil as a deliberate turning away from Good (or from God). One wrote of it as "a falling away from goodness". Another suggested that it is "the result of humans acting against their true nature; against conscience and the human need for acting in the best interest of the group". A further idea was that it is "as far away from God as we can be. ... At heart those committing evil know that, but choose it anyway." And finally evil is "an absence of love, goodness, beauty – evil is based on lack, often masking deep pain and ignorance".

## Evil as a human characteristic

More than half of the respondents believed that evil is a human characteristic, and they explained this in different ways. One commented: "Evil is part of human be-ing, rooted in myth. It is part of the expression of humanity in the world. This means that evil is both expressed and understood within the context of human time." Some believed that "Everyone has the capacity for evil, and our humanity and morality are critical in quashing this." One (male) respondent reflected: "Whatever we want to call it, there are inclinations in almost all of us towards self-serving and egotistical actions, as well as occasional inclinations in many of us (perhaps especially men) towards destructive behaviour. These inclinations can cause great harm to others."

This idea of people being free to choose whether or not to do evil was commented on by several respondents. One explained: "Alone (as far as we are aware) among species we have the capacity to identify right from wrong and to plan our actions. Evil results from a refusal or failure to consider the adverse results of our actions on others." Another called it "the deliberate act of hurting another human, animal, or the natural environment when there is a choice not to". One person suggested that "it may be a result of a series of choices, possibly in practice no more than a drift in the direction of dissonance with the natural order of the universe and/or a reluctance to imagine ourselves in the place of other people/ beings/ animals." Another thought that it was a more deliberate process, calling evil "the deliberate, conscious denial of the infinite worth of every individual being; and the deliberate, conscious exploitation of the planet's irreplaceable resources".

## How people become 'evil'

Many participants were interested in the question of how people become evil. Unlike those quoted above, these people believed that nobody is inherently evil – yet, due to various factors, they commit evil acts. Several suggested reasons for this move away from innate goodness. Some believed that it may be for mental-health or genetic reasons. One commented: "Evil is a human act, usually demonstrated by people whose brains have not had the chance to develop as they should – maybe due to poor parenting, upbringing traditions which are damaging to a developing child, illness, abuse, lack of love, mental illness, poor nutrition, etc." Some stressed the importance of teaching ethical standards to children. One commented: "Most evil acts seem to stem from a failure to understand and empathise with the victim(s), which I think are traits that can be instilled during a person's upbringing." Another wrote: "People are capable of good or evil. They for the most part need moral guidance, which for many is supplied by religion." However, some stated views similar to that of this particular respondent, who suggested: "We need contrast, including between good and evil, to help us develop and grow spiritually, and to gain greater self-knowledge."

Others suggested that evil was the outcome of outside influences. One commented: "Imperfection is a necessary condition of existence. Some people are so damaged by their upbringing and other influences and events, or by illness and fear, that they do evil things." Another wrote: "People who harm others have been damaged emotionally in their lives or are acting from the very fearful part of themselves." Yet others saw evil as "behaviour born out of mental anguish/ pain/ illness"; or stated that "life-alienating actions are a tragic expression of unmet needs". One called it "a state of mind or condition where absolute denial of kindness, honesty, altruism, compassion, love results in deliberate acts of cruelty, suffering, deprivation, torture etc. with no apparent sense of guilt or remorse in the perpetrator(s)". One respondent reflected: "It seems as though it is an absence of compassion. A total unawareness of the God within. It seems strange that a person can be very cruel and sadistic towards one person and yet appear loving and kind to another."

**Some definitions of evil actions**
Some respondents attempted to define which actions they considered to be evil. These included uncontrolled anger towards people and animals; misuse of power; not knowing the difference between coercion and volition; intolerance; abuse of others; acts of violence; barbaric acts of cruelty. In other words, "any harm that is caused due to lack of respect for the sacredness of life". One suggested that evil can also be institutionalised: "for example, in economic systems that funnel all the wealth upwards to a fortunate few, rather than spreading it out evenly so that all can participate. In economic systems which depend on endless growth on a finite planet. It's institutionalised in political systems which deny a voice to some, while amplifying the voice of others."

## *Unitarians views on the 'concept of sin'*

Respondents were asked: "What does the concept of sin mean to you?" The most common responses are summarised in the shared comments below.

### 'Sin' as an irrelevant, outdated, unhelpful concept
Eleven respondents stated outright that they did not believe in the concept of sin. Others found sin outdated, misleading, or meaningless as a concept: a word that they would not use about themselves or anyone else. One stated: "I believe sin is an unhelpful concept, because it's loaded with Judaeo-Christian implications." Another suggested: "It is not enabling to label people as sinners."

### Rejection of the concept of 'original sin' (or not)
More than 20 participants specifically rejected the Christian concept of original sin. One stated firmly: "I absolutely hate and repudiate the idea of 'original sin'." Another explained: "Although I have studied history and theology and intellectually understand the concept, I just don't believe in original sin. I think that the default setting of the universe is neutral or good, and that the divine is nurturing and compassionate." Two people did, however, find some meaning in the term 'original sin'. One wrote: "I am inclined to believe that we suffer from original sin, in that we follow our survival instincts or follow only our own personal interests. This can lead us into a life of selfishness."

### Sin as a control mechanism invented by religions
Several respondents would concur with the participant who saw sin as "a mechanism of control invented by Christianity and other religions". One called it "a mechanism for causing guilt and exercising power and control over the 'guilty'". Another described it as "a human construct. It provokes guilt and loathing in human beings and in many ways is a very destructive concept that destroys people. This has been played out most powerfully in relation to human sexuality. The concept has ground people into dust. That in itself is evil." Others wrote of its capability to "cause much unnecessary misery"; to "blight lives" as "a religious device to create fear and subsequent obedience to a religious hierarchy". One stated:

> *Sin is a useless and destructive concept which is unnecessarily enslaving people in a doctrine of slavish obedience that only serves those in control.*

*Like evil, it is a lazy person's method of control, with very low cost to the controller, and a heavy price for the controlled.*

One person, however, suggested that "Sin is an overused term in Christian churches and overly ignored outside them. Sin is falling short. It is not useful to bracket it with evil. However, we do often need to be forgiven and to forgive ourselves. We need a word that covers those things for which we do need to be forgiven." Another agreed, writing: "I think we do have tendencies to sin and evil, and it is a religious task to overcome them, with others if possible."

**Sin as being out of alignment with God**
One participant explained being 'out of alignment' thus: "Sin hurts God, because it hurts the person/ creature we trespass against, and the God that dwells in them." Another called it "a theological concept defined as any thought or action that endangers the ideal relationship between an individual and God". A third suggested that it is "the name I give to those aspects of myself that close me off from God – that block me from being in the divine flow of love – that stand in the way of my usefulness to my fellows – that close my heart". One person suggested that "Sin is ... part of being human, being broken. To accept that it is a part of us is to accept that we are born into the human world complete with the burdens of its, at times, oppressive and violent history."

**Sin as 'missing the mark' or 'falling short'**
The phrases 'missing the mark' and 'falling short' were used over and over again in the responses to this question. One person explained: "To sin is simply to fall short of the best we can be. We are all sinners in this respect... When we are born, we are pure, without sin. That said, it doesn't take long before we begin to fall short. This does not mean there is anything wrong with us, quite the opposite actually." Another suggested: "No human being is perfect – we all miss the mark and fall short of perfection. ... To atone for our sins, we must apologise to those affected and, if possible, make reparations." And finally: "I think we sin when we do just miss the mark.

We fall short of the beings we could be. We have to reconcile ourselves to ourselves, to God, to each other. I don't believe that we have to have any sort of grand atonement and I don't believe that we get damned to hell for sin."

### Sin as 'going against one's conscience' or 'wrong-doing'

Here there is a more secular approach, with phrases such as 'going against what we believe to be right', and words like 'wrong-doing' . One person suggested: "On the human level, I would class actions which are contrary to the perceived ideal order for human living as 'wrongdoing', 'shortcoming', 'misdemeanour', or, for more serious acts, 'crime against humanity'." Another suggested that sin is about "going against our own nature or against our own culture. It's not wrong in an absolute sense, but it divides us against ourselves and our community."

A few favoured a Buddhist approach to sin, explained by one person thus: "I prefer an ethical approach and the Buddhist idea of Right Thinking, Right Action etc." Another wrote: "Sin to me is the wilful commitment of any hurtful thought, word or deed to others, or my own soul, through weakness to resist natural but unhealthy desires."

### Sin as offending against societal or cultural rules

Some respondents wrote about sin in terms of "a breaking of rules – perhaps the rules of a religion, or your own rules"; or as "a cultural concept which is based on social mores and values which change with time". A few suggested that for this reason it is a value judgement. One warned: "Sin is a social construct; how sin is judged requires consideration and analysis." It was suggested that it "can mean different things in different cultures, times and societies; e.g. it may be sinful to steal, but if you are starving, stealing food may be the only choice". Another specifically rejected the concept of a 'religious sin', writing: "For example, many believers view same-sex relationships as sinful – and so therefore wrong – and yet if two people love each other, where is the harm?" And finally: "Our social norms and beliefs shape our conscience to some extent, while genuine compassion and empathy shape the rest. I think we should seek to nurture a reasoned conscience and make choices based on that."

**Sin as relational dysfunctionality**
By some sin was perceived (in the words of one respondent) as being about "relational dysfunctionality, be that our relationship with our self, others, or the earth". Sin is understood in terms of harming others – other people, other living beings, the living planet. This was explained by one person thus: "Sin is when people do bad things for their own gratification without consideration of the impact their actions might have on other people." Another suggested that this happened "as a result of lack of awareness of our interconnectedness and our divinity".

## *Unitarian views about personal salvation*

Respondents were asked: "What do you believe about personal salvation?" More than half did not answer, rejected the concept, were unsure about it, were negative about it, or thought it was about religious manipulation. The rest described it in one of three ways: in (broadly) Christian terms; in other faith terms; or in 'this life' terms. The main categories of responses are summarised in the shared comments below.

**Personal salvation an outdated, meaningless, irrelevant concept**
Thirty-one respondents (12 per cent) chose not to answer this question. A further 74 (29 per cent) did not believe in the concept of personal salvation. Some just denounced it in a few words: "outdated", "meaningless", "irrelevant"; but others explained their rejection of it. One called it "an erroneous concept, linked to original sin". Another wrote: "I don't think we can be 'saved', because I don't believe in heaven and hell – I'm really not sure about any of the beliefs about us 'getting closer to God'."

**Unsure what 'personal salvation' means**
Those who were not sure about it, or did not understand it, said so briefly or attempted to puzzle it out. One wrote: "What are we being saved from? Doing wrong? I don't know what I think." Another stated: "I do not understand this concept. It usually claims that one has either been absolved

from a supposed sin or has been specifically chosen to receive spiritual awareness that is in fact available to everyone."

### Personal salvation as a form of religious manipulation
Those who believed that it was a form of religious manipulation were forthright about their rejection of it. One wrote: "Salvation is an entirely artificial concept, originating in one of the most dangerous myths ever dreamed up – the Adam and Eve story. What possible logic can there be in a God trapping his creatures in a situation from which he needs to save them?" Another suggested: "The thought of an ultimate 'judgement day' caused much unhappiness to people in the past. All part of the fear agenda of the Judaeo-Christian tradition." Some specifically rejected the Christian doctrine of atonement. One wrote: "I am responsible for my own sins and my own salvation. I utterly deny the Christian notion of the Atonement. I refuse to believe in a God who could require the torture and death of his own son."

### A broadly Christian understanding of personal salvation
Some participants shared a broadly Christian understanding of the concept. Of these, by far the most numerous (16: 6 per cent) were those who had a Universalist understanding of salvation. One explained: "There is no need of salvation. Nobody has to 'rescue' our souls. We are all destined to be, one way or another, united with God. After all, God is [about] infinite love and forgiveness."

Some thought of salvation in terms of "union with God". One wrote of "return to the Universal Soul". Another commented: "I believe that the part of us which is made up of Love will continue after death. This is why all faiths agree that Love is the only important thing." A third wrote: "When we approach God, we encounter all the good and evil of our lives – we are moved to repentance and thus salvation." A small number of participants had a more classically Christian understanding of the concept of personal salvation. One suggested that "anyone who accepts Jesus as their saviour and loves God will be saved". A few wrote of it in terms such as "a reward for striving to live well". One hoped that "if I live as good a life as I possibly can, and make the most of all the opportunities which present themselves, I will proceed to a better world after I die." Another commented: "I remember the dead in my prayers. I would like to think that we shall meet again, and be able to recognise one another and relate to one another."

### Personal salvation in the teachings of other faith traditions

Some respondents had views about personal salvation which owed more to the teachings of other faith traditions. Several had a Buddhist/Hindu understanding of salvation. For example, one person affirmed: "When by your own free choices with the help of the Divine, of the great souls whom the Divine brings into your life to help you, and your friends and loved ones who travel some of your spiritual journey with you, you achieve Enlightenment after some of many physical human lives, you thereby free yourself from karmic compulsions. Then you ascend to one of the high realms where liberated souls live." Another wrote that "this life is just a stage in a very lengthy process of 'becoming', which extends over many lifetimes".

### Personal salvation as something which happens in this life

The most commonly supported understanding of personal salvation, among those respondents who did not completely reject the idea, was that it is something which happens in this life, here on Earth. One stated: "Personal salvation can happen in this life, at any moment, and is something to be celebrated." Another wrote: "Salvation occurs every day as we are saved from the worst aspects of our potential humanity and aim to be the best that we can be." A third reflected: "Like the Unitarians of old, I believe we are saved through our character." Some mentioned the link to the Latin *"salve"*, meaning health, and wrote about personal salvation in terms of spiritual health: "a state of heaven on earth when we are in vital, healthy connection with the earth and the spirit". One wrote: "I think it's more about fulfilment of our potential, finding purpose, within whatever lifespan we may have. Which is for us to set about and work at."

Some people wrote of the need for grace in this process. One explained: "For me, personal salvation is about asking God for help and doing my best to love myself and others. It is about being honest with God when

I feel I'm acting from a non-loving place, and asking for guidance with this." Another wrote: "I believe we can commit ourselves time and again to becoming better people, to serving our neighbour and God; that when we see the shadow, we can turn around to see the sun. But I also see Grace as real – that we occasionally, and for no known reason, receive forgiveness when it sounds like the most foolish, unreasonable choice."

Many described what personal salvation in this life meant to them. The definitions here are a representative sample:

- "To try to have good morals, be honest, caring, sharing, selfless and helpful."
- "Being true to oneself, and living with integrity."
- "Becoming a better person so that by the end of your life you can leave this world contented."
- "Becoming aware of the spiritual nature of humanity, myself, and having a sense that life is more than simply satisfying the body and having a good time."
- "It relates to the here and now. Finding the right path for you to live your life, that allows you to be yourself, be really you, and live a good, unselfish life. To become more compassionate and loving and accept yourself as you are."
- "Salvation is an archetypal concept that each person may define for themselves – it can be interpreted humanistically, for example as recovery or revival after devastating loss, finding purpose in life through love, etc."

Some people suggested that personal salvation may occur at a turning point in human lives. One wrote: "I would use this word to describe something which pulls someone out of a bad place ... more of a trigger for an internal change than the change itself." Others explained it in terms of finding "personal peace". One wrote of "feeling nurtured and surrounded by love from an unexplained source". Another explained: "In a non-Christian context, I interpret salvation as freedom from guilt, possession of a mind at rest with itself, honour intact, all debts paid, no issues left unresolved, contentment with one's lot." Another was "more comfortable with an understanding of it as healing, wholeness and peace with oneself".

There were some cautionary comments, such as "[It] is a state of mind that can be brought about by influences experienced either in solitary conditions, chemical effects or through 'crowd effects'." One person was "not really sure whether we are free agents; genes, environment all play their part in how we turn out. Good and bad may be constructs." Another suggested that "If humans are responsible for their own personal salvation, then it is enough to make anyone neurotic. It potentially exacerbates guilt and remorse when you fall short of your own expectations of what a 'good' person can be." Finally, one person suggested: "All people have the capacity to choose how to live, whether to save themselves when required or to go on as they are."

## *Summary of findings*

Respondents' views of the nature of evil were sometimes complex and almost always carefully nuanced. Some believe that the term 'evil' is not helpful, and others that a distinction needs to be made between natural disasters and human-made ones. Some see evil as a human construct, used to control others, while others perceive it as a separate, active force in the world, in opposition to good. And it is seen by some as a deliberate turning away from good, or God. The most common perception, shared by more than half of the participants, was that evil is a human characteristic, and they explained this in various ways. Some described it as part of the human condition, and believe that everyone has the capacity to do evil things. Others believe that no-one is born evil, but that various factors cause people to turn to evil: for example, environment, upbringing, or mental-health problems.

The views expressed about sin were equally complex. For some, sin is about humankind's relationship with God; for others, it is more about human behaviour: about 'wrongdoing', 'breaking the rules', or 'relational dysfunctionality' – although of course there may be some overlap between these. Some believe that the concept of sin is a harmful one, designed by religions to control and manipulate people, but others find it a helpful guide to behaviour.

The final question explored understandings about personal salvation. A significant number of participants (31: 12 per cent) did not respond to this question. Of those who did, some see it as an outdated, meaningless, and irrelevant concept; some are unsure of the meaning, and others perceive it as a form of religious manipulation. The remaining participants described personal salvation in one of three ways: in (broadly) Christian terms; in other faith terms (mainly Buddhist/Hindu); and in a humanistic "this life" way: a process of spiritual growth which happens during the ordinary human lifespan. This latter concept was the one most commonly shared.

It is clear that the concepts of evil, sin, and personal salvation are important to most respondents, but they are interpreted in many different ways. Most demonstrated an underlying belief in the innate goodness of human beings.

## *Questions for reflection and group discussion*

1. *What do you believe about the nature of evil in the world?*

2. *What does the concept of sin mean to you?*

3. *What do you believe about personal salvation?*

# Chapter 11
# Unitarians and mysteries beyond reason

*The certainty for which we crave*
*No mortal ones can ever know;*
*Uncharted waters we must brave,*
*And face whatever winds may blow.*

John Andrew Storey, *Hymns for Living*, 162

The other two questions in this section of the survey concerned life after death, and intangible phenomena such as fate, karma, and grace. Respondents were asked the following two questions:

- What do you believe happens after we die?
- What are your views about supernatural influences in the world, e.g. fate, karma, grace?

## Unitarian views about life (or not) after death

Life after death – whether there is one, and if so, what form it might take – is one of those questions to which there is no certain answer. As one person commented drily: "No idea. I haven't died yet (or if I have, I've no recollection of the previous life)." But most respondents had a view (or more than one) about this mystery, and these are summarised in the shared comments below.

## Death is the end of everything
Forty-eight people (19 per cent) believed that there is no life after death. Some commented very briefly; for example, "Nothing. We rot." And "We did not exist before conception, and we will not exist after death." Others were more philosophical. One wrote: "Nothing. The lights go out. I am happy with that. I thought I would not be, but somehow I am now happy that nothing is permanent (Buddhist thought) and why worry. Also my brain is too small to decode the universe – so why waste energy on it? I learned this through Unitarianism."

Another commented: "Death is final. I cannot conceive of any kind of continuing existence. My spiritual self is not separate from my physical self; I am a mortal unity." Another wrote simply: "We cease to exist. What a relief!"

## Life before death is more important
A few participants commented that it is "life before death" which is important. One wrote: "The important thing is to be the best person you can before you die, whether or not it might have consequences afterwards." Another wrote: "I believe that the journey through life is all important and that the destination is unimportant."

## We cannot know what happens after death
More than one-third of respondents either admitted straight out that they did not know if there would be life after death, or hoped that there might be, but were not sure what form, if any, it might take. The people who declared that they did not know were generally not concerned by this fact. Typical responses included the following: "I don't know what happens after death and therefore am not interested in formulating a belief system based on lack of information"; and "I hope that we become part of the Great Energy. If we don't, then I won't know about it and I won't much care."

Some respondents had a strong desire to believe in an afterlife. One wrote: "My beliefs on this change on a weekly basis. I would like to believe in some kind of spiritual existence after death. Or that my memories would be passed down with my DNA. ... I wish I was more sure – it would make my life have meaning and make us less frightened of death." Another commented:

"I would like to believe in an afterlife in which all evil has been washed away and all sins forgiven, but I have no proof. I find death very difficult to contemplate because of this lack of specific belief – my own death is not a huge worry, but the death of others presents me with great problems."

## What happens to our bodies after death

Quite a number of participants focused on the physical realities of death. One hoped "that when I die I'll break down into the earth and continue in the natural cycle that I work with as a gardener". Another commented that they and their partner had chosen to be buried rather than cremated when they die, because "That way at least our bodies will provide some good to the earth, rather than adding to the carbon already in the atmosphere."

Some believed that, as our bodies are made up of atoms, they will be "returned to the cosmos". One explained this in scientific terms: "We are biochemical engines. When we die that decays, and certain indestructible atoms and elements are released back into the universe in accordance with the first law of thermodynamics." Another commented: "We become a collection of particles of matter and join the life of the earth, and therefore we never leave the planet, our home. ... Energy is never lost, we are told." A third suggested: "Our atoms regroup into millions of different organisms, so we are all reincarnated in a sense."

Some saw this as a spiritual process: "I think my warmth and energy and force goes to the Source and is ready to be used again." Another commented: "Our energy bodies go back into the universe energy field, ready to go on the next journey of life in this universe." A third believed that "our 'miraculous', temporary, unique arrangement of 'atoms' returns into the stuff of the universe".

## We live on in the experiences and memories of others

Quite a number of respondents believed that one lives on "in the memories of one's loved ones" and friends. One suggested: "Any concept of eternal life is in the memories I have left in the minds of those who knew me, and any changes in the universe which my being on the earth has made. Everyone leaves an intangible 'imprint' on the universe, so that it is not the same as if they had not lived." Another commented: "The best we can hope for is that we have made a contribution to the good life, appreciated and celebrated the gift of life, and will be remembered, for a while." These responses showed an acceptance of the universe as it is, of human lives as they are, and of the transitory nature of all things.

### The soul/spirit lives on after death

Then there were those who believed in some kind of spiritual after-life. Thirty-three (13 per cent) believed that the "soul" or "spirit" "carries on" in some way. One explained: "I don't believe that death is an end and that there is nothing else afterwards. I think that there is a change of state or consciousness that we don't understand, and that the soul or spirit is eternal." Another put this in more philosophical terms: "I do not believe that mind is an epiphenomenon of matter; mind is the source of everything – 'in the beginning was the word'. So physical death need not mean the death of consciousness or the death of the essential 'I'. I think there is sufficient evidence that some part of an individual consciousness lives on after physical death."

Some believed that the soul or spirit moves to a different 'plane' after death. One explained: "We go to a 'plane' at which our spiritual selves already 'are'. That we continue our spiritual evolving path towards the infinite." Another wrote simply: "I believe we all have an eternal self – call it a soul or fifth-dimensional being that is beyond time and space."

Some wrote of their hope of meeting loved ones in another life. One wrote: "I would like to think that something of us (the soul?) lasts and can be reintegrated with loved ones." Another believed in a sort of spiritual reincarnation: "I'd like to think that I will have another life and meet the same souls/ spirits/ people next time round."

One respondent shared a profound personal experience: "Witnessing my mother's very peaceful and lovely death had a profound effect on me. She talked us through what she could 'see', telling us that we have nothing to fear and that she was going to a lovely place. ... I think I do now believe that something of people's spirit lives on and joins a well of 'good consciousness'." A few participants shared this belief in the soul's translation to a 'better place'. One wrote: "I believe we live on in spiritual form, not too far away from who and where we are now. Rejoining the whole, which is God. Also having to account for our life and deeds, to ourselves and God, as one."

This belief in a broadly Christian 'heaven' was shared by another, who commented: "I choose to believe that as/after people die, they realise the impact of their lives for good and bad. ... I choose to believe people are in a timeless state of peace, comfort, love, safety and forgiveness." Others disagreed. One commented: "I imagine that few Unitarians believe in an afterlife involving a Heaven and Angels." Another wrote: "I do not have a concept of heaven or hell where some almighty God presides, rather an ongoing of the soul in some form."

Some believed that "the soul, which came from God, will return to God". One explained it this way: "I believe we inherit a soul from the Universal Soul when we are conceived/ born, and when we die, our soul returns to the Universal Soul." Another believed "that we rejoin God in the sense that we rejoin the loving universal energy at the heart of everything". A third wrote of it in more abstract terms, saying: "I think when we die we return to Reality. Life on Earth is a short interlude in order to learn and experience and grow, and then we return to where we really belong."

Others wrote of it as a merging "into the universal consciousness of the creative Universe". One explained: "I think that consciousness is an inherent potential in all matter, and so when the atoms get shuffled and re-appear in another form (animal, vegetable or mineral) they get another go at getting experience of being in a different setting." One respondent expressed similar ideas:

> *As an organism here, our psyche is pre-written into the universe before we were born and will continue to be written into the universe after we die. That is because time means nothing except to us who live through it. Each of us is like a set of beads forming part of an abacus. When we cease to exist as separate individuals, the beads on the abacus still exist in the same sequence, but they are moved about differently and mean different things. There is no continuation of us as an individual experience.*

Another wrote: "My faith guides me to think that we join a larger consciousness. [Using a] river analogy ... perhaps we decay in the waters of God, dissolving into [which] we too flow perpetually with the stream." Another also used a river metaphor, suggesting: "It is comforting to think that our lives are like rivers and at the end of our lives we join the infinite ocean of God's love. Whether we maintain our individual identities or not, I cannot say. It is enough to know that our destiny is Love."

### Life after death in reincarnation

Another group expressed belief in reincarnation of some kind. One wrote: "The moment the physical body dies, the soul is released into another world, which is close to the physical world all the time, and the soul goes on to its next journey, possibly coming back into a human body in the future, possibly not." Another suggested: "I feel it's likely that our souls reincarnate. I have read some convincing arguments towards it, and it feels logical. I feel that some people are old souls and new souls, and I feel it would go some way to explaining personality, as well as things like our natural affinities for certain people (in combination with our evolved abilities to make judgements etc)."

Some stated their belief in karmic reincarnation. One wrote: "Buddhist/Hindu sort of thinking – our soul/spiritual essence is transmuted into a new life form, whether that be human, angel, demon, etc., depending on overall karma levels. This is to continue the long process of escaping the cycle of existence, back to the pure consciousness – God." Another wrote:: "I do believe that we reap what we sow – not in a hell-fire and damnation sense – but in some kind of karmic sense – perhaps we're reborn and whatever we didn't learn we have to go through again in another incarnation?"

## *Unitarian views about supernatural influences*

Respondents were asked: "What are your views about supernatural influences in the world, e.g. fate, karma, grace?" On reflection, a better wording than "supernatural influences" might have been "intangible phenomena". Twenty-five respondents chose not to answer this question; the responses of the rest are summarised in the shared comments below.

**Supernatural influences do not exist**
More than one-fifth of all respondents stated outright that they did not believe in supernatural influences. Some, such as this one, were content merely to state their (non)belief: "I don't believe in them, and the concepts don't occupy my thoughts." Another wrote: "Supernatural? Natural is super enough." Another professed belief in "rational explanations, not supernatural influences" – echoed by another, who stated: "The world is material. Whatever happens is caused by nature or human agency." Another suggested that "These ideas can be harmful. I have seen problems caused by superstitions."

**Open-minded about the existence of supernatural influences**
Another group (31: 12 per cent) did not dismiss the idea of supernatural influences outright, but were willing to keep an open mind about it. One commented: "It would be a brave man to deny their existence, but I personally have never experienced them." Some approached them cautiously. One wrote: "I don't dismiss them but I don't just blindly believe in them. I try to use my reason and logical thinking." Another professed to be "open to the ideas. I don't pin hope on them or have great faith in them. [But] I do feel energy and so I know that 'something' is there, but what exactly I don't know."

Some participants opted for a rational approach. One wrote: "We don't know what we don't know. So we try to explain it through our limited understanding. There's a whole other strata of understanding and experience of our world which we may never access. We'll never understand it all. It's like trying to see colours outside our human viewing spectrum – our senses are too limited to see it. Other animals have different senses to detect and 'read' the world which we don't have – our senses can only detect a tiny amount of input – this is the supernatural."

Another expressed a similar view: "Sometimes the universe blesses us and sometimes it doesn't. Bad things happen to good people. That's life, the way of the world. Unlooked-for and undeserved good fortune also happens. You might describe these as grace or fate, but these are just our ways of explaining things to ourselves and trying to make sense." A third put belief in supernatural influences down to "wishful thinking".

### Supernatural influences are a mystery beyond rational explanation
A third group (41: 16 per cent) believed that supernatural influences were a mystery beyond rational explanation, but accepted that they did exist. One suggested: "Very occasionally, the laws of science seem to bend, reminding us that there are limitations to rationality. Pascal puts it better: the supreme achievement of Reason is to realise that there is a limit to Reason." Some mentioned being "open to the possibilities and mysteries of life". One gave a personal example: "I know as a capable 'water diviner' that there is as yet no scientific explanation as to the mechanism, or source of the actual force."

One person suggested: "These are human words that express the mystery of divine activity and experience in and out of the world. Whether these are supernatural, supranatural or natural, I couldn't answer." Another quoted Tennyson, writing:

> I believe that 'more things are wrought by prayer than this world dreams of' and that things once deemed 'supernatural' i.e. healing, answers to prayers, synchronicity, psychic phenomena, are in fact natural laws that we're only just discovering. That doesn't negate for me the possibility that a divine presence is behind it all – rather that his/her/its intervention in the world is governed and limited by laws not yet understood. In a post-Newtonian world, I think Unitarians have a lot of catching up to do, i.e. recognising the interface between spirituality and the findings of quantum physics etc.

### General comments about supernatural influences
A number of respondents made more general comments about supernatural influences. One explained them as agents of "a universal consciousness that lures life to be the best it can be". Another had a somewhat different view, writing: "Basically, I am the hands, heart and active body for G-D; the supernatural works if I am willing to do the job."

Thirteen people had no strong views either way, and stated this. A few respondents (8: 3 per cent) had no doubts at all. One wrote: "Supernatural influences are more abundant than particles, they are flowing within and through and around us all the time. Each one of us is never truly separated from the Divine of which we are a part, though we may for a while fall under the illusion that we are."

Many respondents shared their beliefs about one or more of the three examples given in the question: fate, karma, and grace. The rest of this chapter will deal with each of these in turn.

**Fate as a supernatural influence**

Opinions on the phenomenon of fate were divided. Twenty-one respondents (8 per cent) did not believe in it; three expressed a caveat concerning free will; 22 (8 per cent) believed in it; and a further six wrote about 'luck or circumstance'.

One person who did not believe in fate wrote: "I don't believe in fate or the intervention of the Divine in individual lives as such – I think the universe is too random for that." Another commented: "I believe human beings might perceive events as 'fated', but I don't believe such external influences exist. If so, logically we would have to hate God for the extraordinary suffering endured by the innocent."

Others believed that the concept of fate is contrary to human free will. One wrote: "I don't believe in fate or determinism. I believe that we have freewill. No-one can escape personal moral responsibility on the grounds that what they did was pre-determined. We can be grateful for good fortune, which is a matter of chance." Another commented: "As I see it, the concept of Fate is a denial of free will, a sense of responsibility and the idea of making choices."

Another had a slightly different view: "I believe that when you are ready, things happen. ... A great many things have happened to me that could be explained by fate, but when I analyse them, it was because I had already been thinking about them and my unconscious mind was preparing for them, so that when I saw the opportunity I was looking for and took it, it seemed to be 'fate'. I had set myself on that path."

Those who believed in fate explained it in terms of predestination, and recognition of inevitability. One wrote: "I believe that there are moments and relationships that feel deeply 'meant to be', and we must aim to find and be all we can be in life." Some were quite fatalistic; one wrote: "Everything happens for a reason, and every person you cross paths with was there for a reason. You can't change what the universe has planned out for you." Another had "a sense that this moment couldn't possibly be any different from the way it is, and that the universe is unfolding the way it must. You might call that fate."

More than one wrote of 'signs' in their lives. One explained: "I believe that things happen for a reason and that life experiences always provide learning experiences. I believe in signs that are sent to guide us in daily life. I believe that by asking the universe in times of need that you will be given signs to help, you find what you need."

Some wrote of the influence of luck or circumstance in human lives. One commented:

*It is true that some people have 'luck'. Life deals them a fair hand. How is that? I've had my share of suffering the consequences of bad decisions; of being deeply unhappy. I know that my involvement with the Unitarians in the UK made a huge difference ... something was missing till then. What's all that about? Maybe the opportunity to reflect on what is really important; to be brought into contact with people and inspirational words?*

### Karma as a supernatural influence

Quite a number of participants had a view about karma. One wrote: "My favourite description of karma is that by acting out of kindness you gain a share in a kinder world; by acting out of hate you gain a share in a more hateful world." Another was not sure it was a supernatural influence, but suggested: "It's more about cultivating positive good attitudes, motives, and behaviour and openness of mind that directly or indirectly lead to more good." Another wrote: "What goes around, comes around – so I try not to give out anything that I would not expect to get back."

One used an analogy from art to describe karma:

*It's like we all have a section of canvas to paint on during our lifetime. We can choose whether to paint with grace and colour, or we can destroy it with dark splodges. At the end of our lives we get to see the entire canvas, and how our little part has affected the whole. If I cause harm to someone, I create a dark splodge on their canvas as well as my own. This has an effect on the whole painting. So I don't believe in karmic debt, but I believe that our actions come back to us, because if we create a more positive world then we get to live in it.*

Other respondents were unsure about karma. One wrote: "I know that you reap what you sow. But I also know that bad things happen to good people, and good things happen to bad people. So I don't know." Another wrote: "The famous text, 'as a person reaps, so shall [they] sow', is an excellent ethical, spiritual, and practical maxim, but there are 'hard cases' where sometimes such principles are hard to discern in the working out of events."

**Grace as a supernatural influence**
Perhaps the most complex set of responses in this section were respondents' beliefs about the nature of grace. Some saw it as an active force in the world. One wrote: "I think grace can be active in the world if people (and for all we know other animals too) choose to channel it. I think the Divine seeks to ensure the ongoing flourishing of creation, including the general fostering over time of more open, compassionate ways of living, because that is its nature." Another put it this way:

*I believe in the interconnectedness of all things and people, and within that the working of a 'flow' which might be called Divinity (or Holy Spirit). Prayer and positive (or negative!) thinking interact with this with noticeable effect. I think that maintaining the right connection and interaction with this 'flow' is what is probably what is meant by being in a 'state of grace'.*

Some spoke of grace as a sense of being held by God. One called it "the loving support we get from the Divine". Others saw grace as God's intervention in our lives. One wrote: "I also believe in divine grace – that God can intervene in our lives by nudging us in the right direction." For another, it meant "One is more likely to recognise or be able to accept opportunities, gifts when they appear – which is what I understand by grace." A third wrote of "divine presence – a flow of grace", and another remarked: "The winds of grace are always blowing, but we have to put up the sails." One commented simply: "Miracles happen."

For some, grace was experienced as a reward or blessing. One wrote: "Grace – in the sense of unearned blessings – happens all the time." Another suggested that "Grace can operate where the person's innermost core is reaching for God." One respondent explained: "All life is grace, in that all life is freely and lovingly given to us, not because we deserve it, but just because of the outrageous goodwill of the Wellspring of Existence." One wondered about people "who do seem to be 'holy' in a way that I cannot reach ... and I wonder if in fact to be 'holy' in the way of these amazing Mother Teresa people is the result of serious and long practice, just like to be a concert pianist is."

## Other supernatural influences

Finally, some respondents mentioned other supernatural influences. Four mentioned serendipity and synchronicity. One commented: "Synchronicity/ serendipity/ good luck seems to happen all the time. I like hearing about instances of it, but I'm not sure it is really supernatural or evidence of 'God's' grace." Another wrote: "I think that there are many examples of coincidence, serendipity, synchronicity which are beyond my understanding but suggest to me influences that are over and above what I can currently comprehend." One respondent revealed: "I have been a student of astrology for half a century. It is the oldest and most persistent belief system of all. .... We moderns consider it a superstition and refuse to engage with it, or even to examine it, because it so completely challenges the materialistic nihilism which dominates our intellectual world. It demonstrates that the universe is not the accidental but pointless outcome of random forces, but that there is purpose behind everything."

## *Summary of findings*

There are some concepts which may best be described as "mysteries beyond reason", because it is not possible to approach them from a purely rational viewpoint. Life after death is one of these, and the existence and power of supernatural influences is another. Participants shared a wide range of views on both these questions.

Their views about the possibility of life after death varied widely. A significant minority (48 people: 19 per cent) declared that they do not believe in it. More than one-third are open-minded about it, but are not sure what form, if any, it might take. Many of these are willing to consider possibilities such as the idea that human beings 'live on' in the memories of others; or that the soul/ spirit lives on after death, perhaps as a return to God, or to the Source; or as life on a spiritual plane or some other form of consciousness; or in a reincarnated existence.

The other question in this chapter sought respondents' views on supernatural influences such as fate, karma, and grace. While a significant minority (more than 20 per cent) of respondents reject the existence of such phenomena, the views of the rest span a wide range. A further 12 per cent do not dismiss them out of hand, but are willing to keep an open mind, while another 16 per cent believe that supernatural influences are a mystery beyond rational explanation, but they accept that they exist.

Quite a few respondents believe in the concept of karma: that our past actions affect us, either positively or negatively, and that our present actions will affect us in the future. Some gave personal examples of how this had worked out in their own lives (as did those who believe in fate). The responses about the phenomenon of grace were more complex. Some see it as an active force in the world; some as a sense of being held by God; others as God's intervention in human lives; or as a reward or a blessing.

Many respondents demonstrated a willingness to engage with 'mysteries beyond reason', which tallies with the responses presented in Chapter 2, in which a majority of respondents commented that although reason is an important part of their Unitarian faith, there are matters beyond reason too.

## *Questions for reflection and group discussion*

1. Is there life after death?
2. Do you believe in the working of supernatural influences, such as fate, karma, or grace, in the world?

# Chapter 12
# Unitarian spiritual practices and activities

*Inward peace and inward living*
*Must be given rightful place,*
*Even though we live in cities,*
*Even as we run the race.*

Bruce Findlow, *Hymns for Living*, 51

The final section of the survey sought to discover what kinds of spiritual practice respondents engaged in, and how often, and what other Unitarian activities they participated in. They were asked the following questions:

- Would you describe yourself as religious, spiritual, both, or neither?
- Do you have a daily spiritual/devotional practice?
- Do you have a weekly spiritual/devotional practice?
- Do you have a less frequent spiritual/devotional practice?
- How important is it to you to have spiritual/devotional practices as part of your life?
- What Unitarian-led activities have you taken part in?
- Which Unitarian societies, if any, are you a member of?

## Religious, spiritual, both, or neither

Respondents were asked whether they would describe themselves as:

- religious, but not spiritual
- spiritual, but not religious
- both religious and spiritual
- neither.

Their responses are shown in Figure 12.1.

Figure 12.1: Religious, Spiritual, Both or Neither

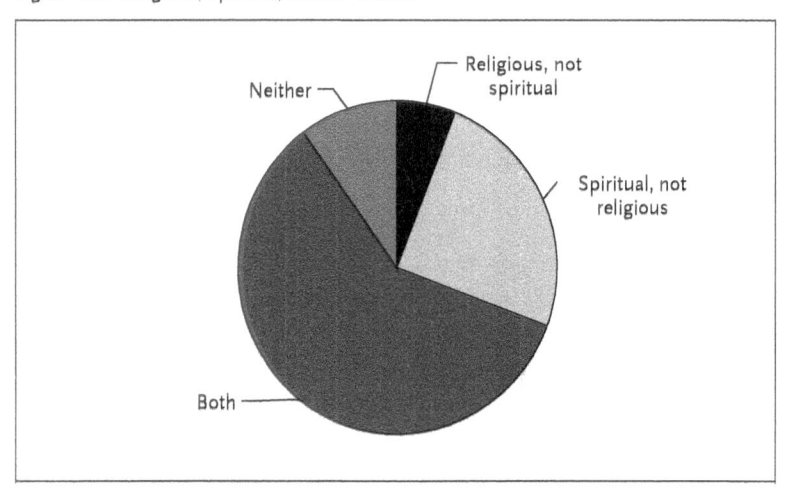

Although a comment box was not provided for this question, some people felt the need to clarify their choice. Six objected that it was difficult to decide without precise definitions of both terms. Some offered their own interpretations, several commenting on the root meaning of the word 'religion' as 'that which binds'. One explained: "I describe myself as religious because I go to be part of a congregation every week, and I like the ritual of it; I occasionally think of myself as spiritual, but am quite uneasy about the term." Another wrote: "I would say I am more spiritual than religious, but I am a bit religious, as in I believe in coming together with others for worship." One participant commented: "I think they are ultimately the same thing, but 'religion' can be misinterpreted when it becomes too authoritarian and judgemental. I feel 'religious' in the sense of to re-link, re-connect with God, which is then spiritual." Another wrote: "Not sure about either of those terms. Compassion and kindness, respecting all life, are what matters to me. Does that make me religious?" Another was "suspicious of spiritual on its own, as it can mean selfish and otherworldly. I am more religious than spiritual, but recognise the life of the spirit as important."

Some owned to being "both to varying degrees". One wrote: "Not religious in the normal sense. I do not follow doctrines that are dictated to me or fixed rules to live by, but I have deep and demanding spiritual aims and I try to live up to them, although I do not manage it all the time, of course."

## *Respondents' daily spiritual/devotional practices*

Respondents were asked whether they had a daily spiritual or devotional practice. Their answers are summarised in the shared comments below.

**Prayer**
More than a quarter of the respondents (66: 26 per cent) had some sort of daily prayer practice, usually first thing in the morning, or last thing at night, or both. One wrote: "I pray every day, morning and evening. In the morning, my prayers focus on my plans for the day ahead, and in the evening, I review the day, apologise for my errors and shortcomings, give thanks for the many blessings I've received." Some called the practice of reviewing their day "meditation" or "reflection", rather than "prayer". Two mentioned saying grace before meals. Others believed that it was important to be in conversation with God. One wrote: "I pray hourly ... I stay as close as I can in communion with God." Another commented: "Conversations with God are part of everything I do. In particular, I ask God's guidance and protection every morning and always give praise and thanks if anything has gone well or I think something is beautiful. I was once told by an elderly nun that you have to repeat prayers so that they can have a heartbeat and live." A third wrote of "a constant inward dialogue with God".

### Meditation/reflection time in silence

Spending time in silence was also important for a significant number of participants (71: 28 per cent). Many described it as meditation, but others described it as "mindful reflection", "contemplation", or "centring prayer". Most did not make comments about this practice, but one mentioned "Silent meditation, sometimes for just a few mins, sometimes longer, to silence the active mind". Another reflected: "I try to meditate for 10/20 minutes each day, because this means my day feels it has begun aright." A third commented: "I try to meditate. This is spiritual and involves connecting to the earth and universe." Five respondents mentioned lighting a candle as part of their prayer or meditation practice.

### Writing and reading practices

A few people (8: 3 per cent) used some form of writing as a spiritual practice. One mentioned the 'Write for your Life' practice;[18] four kept a daily spiritual journal; one did "reflective writing"; and another two had early-morning writing practices. Others (21: 8 per cent) did some spiritual reading daily. One wrote: "I spend time each morning reading (books of prayers, or other writings of spiritual content) and thinking about what I have read." Another commented: "I read some kind of spiritual text most days. These days it is the Bible, especially the Psalms. I try to read one psalm per day."

### Physical practices

Some participants mentioned a variety of physical practices which they found spiritually rewarding. These included yoga, tai chi, reiki, walking, and working on an allotment or gardening. One wrote: "My spiritual practice is part of my walking, cycling and being in the outdoors." Another commented: "I practise yoga daily, which I see as a primarily spiritual practice." A third found spiritual satisfaction in "Walking alone, in silence, or working alone in my garden, trying to absorb myself in the present moment and in what is around me."

---

18  http://www.merlefeld.com, accessed 27 October 2017.

### Reverence for nature
Other respondents also mentioned reverence for nature as a spiritual practice. One wrote: "I always 'greet the day' outside and go out last thing to see stars/ weather etc." A third wrote: "I walk in the forest and commune with nature. I gaze at the sky and think of the wonder of existence and the miracle of life." Another mentioned having "moments every day when I stop to reflect or simply close my eyes and breathe deeply or view the landscape whilst un-focusing from what I am doing".

### Gratitude practices
A number of people (13: 5 per cent) mentioned having a daily gratitude practice. One explained: "I used to have a gratitude practice at bedtime. I have stopped ... because I seem to be grateful all the time now." Another mentioned practising "gratitude for the gift of life, and the gift of the senses". A third wrote: "I just thank God for everything as often as I can, simply by sending out a thought."

### Other daily spiritual practices
The rest mentioned a wide variety of spiritual practices which they found helpful in their daily lives. These included tuning in to spirit guides/ guardian angels; doing art; trying to be accountable in every way; "living within the confines of my spiritual and moral compass"; vegetarianism; dishwashing; Pagan ritual; attunement; tending a shrine or sacred table; and daily 'me' time to recharge the batteries.

### No daily spiritual practice
But nearly half of all the respondents (121: 47 per cent) did not have a daily spiritual or devotional practice. A further 11 did sometimes, but not always. One explained: "I aspire to having a daily spiritual practice and have periods when I succeed in this, but also many periods when I do not succeed." Another wrote: "Sometimes, for a while, especially when life gets difficult. I'm afraid that if I keep it up 'religiously' it will become irksome and kill the authentic perception."

## *Respondents' weekly spiritual/devotional practices*

Respondents were asked whether they had a weekly spiritual or devotional practice. Sixty-nine (27 per cent) said that they did not; another 144 (56 per cent) mentioned weekly attendance at a Unitarian place of worship. Other popular options included some form of meditation, mindfulness, or "quiet time" practice (24: 9 per cent); worship at other churches or Quaker meeting (13: 5 per cent); and physical activities such as yoga, tai chi, qi gong, and being out in nature or gardening (14: 5 per cent).

### Attending a Unitarian worship service

Most of the people who mentioned attending Unitarian worship did not comment further. But a few did. One wrote: "I go to church for inspiration, fellowship, comfort, understanding, and to support it so that it can help and inspire others." Another enjoyed "the sense of community, getting together, taking care of each other. I enjoy the variety of topics covered in the services and the space to think and take time out." One had a different reason for attending: "I like to go to church whenever I can, but this I define as being the opportunity to open my mind and to be among like-minded people who I feel are my community, rather than about devotion."

A few respondents who were worship leaders mentioned that "Sunday worship is a spiritual practice, though it can be difficult when one is leading it. If I'm not leading weekly services, I attend them." Another commented: "Going to church used to be that – until I became a minister. I'm looking to find a replacement."

### Meditation/reflection/time in silence

Some of the people who mentioned weekly meditation or other silent practices also made comments. One wrote: "I like to take quiet time to declutter my mind, think about things, find a calm balance ...". Another did "a walking meditation in the open air at least once a week". Several were members of organised meditation groups, including two who attended Buddhist meditation groups.

### Attending other worship services

Those attending Quaker meetings seemed to alternate between these and Unitarian worship services. Similarly, one wrote: "I like attending Evensong in the evening, but the Unitarians in the morning!" A second commented: "Currently attend Anglican Friday Prayers: a mixture of liturgical worship and open prayer. Attend Anglican Sunday Eucharist where I sing in the choir, but do not say the creed or take communion."

Other choices of places to worship included the Metropolitan Community Church, which one respondent described as "a Christian fully-inclusive church"; "attending Buddhist vespers at temple"; and an inter-faith centre. One respondent commented: "I'm aware of the Jewish Sabbath as I live in a Jewish area; sometimes I join in the service at the synagogue. Also, I go to Christian church services when I can."

### Other weekly spiritual practices

The comments on physical practices, such as yoga, tai chi, qi gong, or being outside in nature, were similar to the ones mentioned in the daily practices above. Other weekly spiritual practices were many and varied: they included participation in communion services; Friday night shabbas prayers and candles; weekly sabbath/ rest day (ministers); writing poetry or journalling; reading; prayer; chanting, both Taizé and other; listening to classical music; "Tao on Tuesdays"; discussion group; art; fasting; recording of dreams with a Jungian therapist; worship via internet or radio; and an hour-long bath.

## *Respondents' less frequent spiritual/devotional practices*

Respondents were asked whether they had a less frequent spiritual or devotional practice. Ninety-seven (35 per cent) said they did not. Others mentioned a huge variety of practices which gave their lives meaning. Popular options (five or more respondents) included:

- Meditation, quiet time
- Unitarian worship

- Celebrating religious feast days/holidays
- Occasional retreats
- Prayer
- Spiritual music or singing
- Communing with nature
- Reading poetry/spiritual works
- Writing, journalling
- Remembrance of loved ones/others
- Various 'New Age' practices.

### Meditation/reflection/time in silence
Those enjoying meditation or quiet time did this both in groups and alone. Participants also wrote about walking meditation, singing meditation, walking a labyrinth, and setting aside times for quiet reflection. One explained:

> *I make myself a cup of strong, loose, fragrant tea or pour a glass of wine. I put some candles on my coffee table and light some incense. Sit comfortably on sofa or on a rug and relax. I then consider this time to be my prayer. I try to connect to God in my thoughts, however profound or human they may be, I don't run away from them. I usually start by saying quietly the Lord's Prayer or listening to sung Lord's Prayer arranged by some contemporary artists.*

Another commented: "At unplanned times, I stop, usually at night outside the city, and meditate on the awe and wonder of my blessed life on this planet and on the appalling cruelty of existence in general."

### Attending a Unitarian worship service
Those who attended Unitarian worship less than weekly usually did so because their congregation met only fortnightly or monthly. One regular worship leader commented: "When not conducting Unitarian worship, I try to attend worship services as a congregant, both in Unitarian churches and other denominations."

## Celebrating religious feast days or holidays

Celebrating religious feast days or holidays was an important spiritual practice for some. One wrote: "I do occasionally celebrate religious feast days/ holidays, either in the Christian calendar or in the Pagan one." Celebrating the eight Pagan festivals was a popular option; eleven of the 16 respondents who mentioned this practice marked these. Of the other five, three mentioned Lent, one mentioned Christmas and Harvest, and the other occasionally attended Buddhist festivals.

## Going on retreat

Going on retreat was another popular spiritual practice for respondents, with 13 saying that they had attended either day retreats, or weekend retreats, or week retreats. Some went with "spiritual companions"; others went alone. One person spent a week with the Iona Community every year. Another attended "retreats (often silent) particularly with the Bede Griffiths sangha, following a daily rhythm based on that in the original BG ashram in India".

## Prayer

Two attended a monthly prayer group, but for most of the respondents who cited prayer it was a less formal process. One wrote: "I pray, to give thanks and ask for support and guidance sometimes." Another commented: "I pray as I feel the need." A third prayed "to give thanks or pray for strength/ courage and for others".

## Music and singing

Listening to music or singing was important to some participants. One explained: "Sometimes, when I'm at home alone, I like to play some music in my living room, be it Zen/ Buddhist meditation music, contemporary music, religious/ Christian music, depending on my mood." Another called listening to music "a constant resource for spiritual enrichment and refreshment". Others preferred active participation: the singing meditation mentioned above was one example. Another commented: "I love singing, especially Taizé or African songs – I find this spiritual when we get it right (I sing in a community choir)."

### Communing with nature
Communing with nature was important for some people. One wrote: "I find spiritual contentment in enjoying the wonders of the natural world." Another mentioned going for long walks in the countryside "in which I take time to stop, admire, appreciate, and give thanks for nature and the world we live in". Another described sometimes being "moved to examine a natural object or phenomenon or rejoice in some aspect of human behaviour".

### Reading and writing practices
Some respondents enjoyed reading poetry or spiritual works. One wrote: "I always have some kind of spiritual book on the go – however loosely that's defined." Others preferred writing, such as this respondent: "I explore spiritual and emotional ideas in quiet-time writing." Another explained: "I have a number of erratic practices. Journaling my prayers is probably the most notable." A third commented: "I have periods where I write, aiming for daily, but not succeeding."

### Remembrance of loved ones
The remembrance of loved ones or others was an important spiritual ritual for some participants. One reported making "an annual trip to the seaside pier where I scattered some of my mother's ashes, the sea also being where my father's ashes are scattered". Another "marks the days when I lost loved ones, and focus on gratitude for their lives". Two others had rituals for "honouring those who have passed on, returned from whence we came. Candles in a quiet place, often by moonlight."

### New Age[19] practices
Various 'New Age' practices were cited by some respondents, including healing hands, cleansing, reliance on energy shields and guardian angels for protection, angel cards and tarot cards, and colour and crystal meditational practices.

---

19   It is appreciated that some of these practices are far older, but as they have been popularised in recent years they are grouped together under the title 'New Age'.

**Other less frequent spiritual practices**
Other less frequent practices were numerous: four people mentioned a regular meeting with a spiritual director; four attended services at other churches; three enjoyed spiritual walking; three visited sacred or holy places; three attended worldwide spiritual gatherings; and three lit candles. Two mentioned attendance at Unitarian Summer School; two were members of Unitarian discussion groups; two were members of women's groups; two did yoga; and two had an irregular gratitude practice.

Spiritual or devotional practices mentioned by only one respondent each included attendance at meetings of the Progressive Christianity Network, the Sea of Faith, and the Theosophical Society; deep breathing under stress; circle dancing; analysis of dreams; communion; tai chi; watching Unitarian or UU sermons on YouTube; membership of a drumming circle (shamanic journeying); meeting with a spiritual teacher; attendance at General Assembly annual meetings; attending FUSE (the annual Festival of Unitarians in the South-East); time in an isolation tank; and space clearing (de-cluttering) of houses. But how important were these many and varied practices to individual respondents? The next question sought to find this out.

## *The importance of spiritual/devotional practices*

Respondents were asked "How important is it to you to have spiritual/devotional practices as part of your life?" and they were offered the following options:

- very important
- fairly important
- I enjoy them when I do them with others, but they are not vital to me
- not very important
- not important at all.

Their responses are shown in Figure 12.2. Five people used phrases such as "fundamental and indispensable" to describe their spiritual practices.

One wrote: "As vital as food and water". Another explained: "Absolutely essential. If I miss my daily devotional practice, it's like missing a meal. It's so easy for me to slip into ego-driven thinking and behaviour if I don't engage in daily prayer or some kind of 'connection' to what I consider to be 'God'."

Figure 12.2: The Importance of Spiritual / Devotional Practices to Respondents (from options supplied)

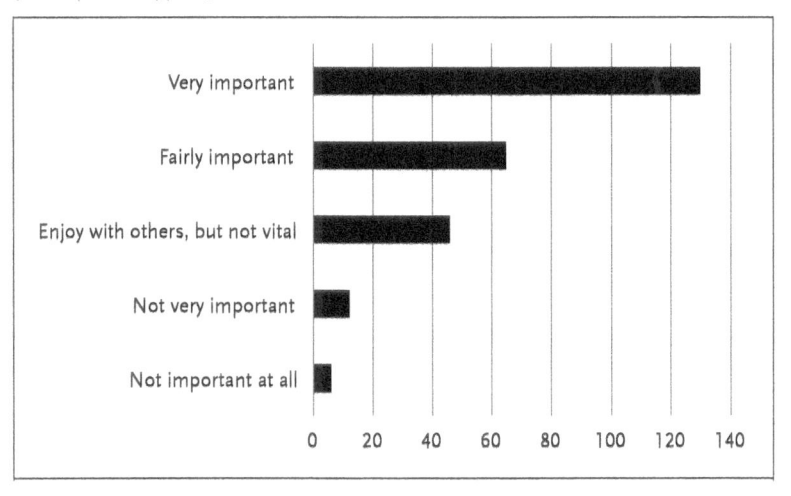

| Category | Count |
|---|---|
| Very important | ~130 |
| Fairly important | ~65 |
| Enjoy with others, but not vital | ~45 |
| Not very important | ~10 |
| Not important at all | ~5 |

Some saw their practices as a part of their daily lives, rather than "a separate, compartmentalised practice". One commented: "It is important. I don't necessarily separate them from ordinary life though. Like Thich Nhat Hanh, I see washing the dishes and housework as part of spiritual practice – along with sharing my day with my partner." This was echoed by the respondent who wrote: "Spiritual practices are integral to my life and I would find it difficult to separate them from my everyday life; e.g. I consider countryside walking, running, and cycling as both physical and spiritual practices." Another commented: "I need something to remind me that I am finite. I need a connection to boost me in life and living morally. It gives me meaning and purpose to go on with life."

Three respondents commented that spiritual or devotional practices were becoming more important as they were getting older. One wrote: "Becoming more important as other activities are having to be given up, or reduced." Another commented: "I have very little going on, so they are becoming more important by default." The third wrote: "Now. They were not in the recent past really."

## *Respondents' participation in Unitarian activities and societies*

The final two questions of the survey asked respondents about their participation in Unitarian activities and societies. They were asked:

- What Unitarian-led activities have you taken part in?
- Which Unitarian societies, if any, are you a member of?

For the first question, respondents were offered a wide range of options. Their responses are shown in Figure 12.3. They clearly demonstrate the importance of other-than-Sunday activities in the lives of the respondents. As might be expected, the particular events attended by them were many and varied, but attendance at the annual 'General Assembly meetings' and 'Social events in church/hall' were the most frequently cited by respondents. The fact that 70 copies of this survey were given out at the 2017 GA annual meetings may have skewed this response.

Even the many options supplied were not sufficient; a significant number mentioned other Unitarian-led activities in which they had participated. One person observed that there were "too many to list", and another cited being "on various committees at Essex Hall". Three participants mentioned attending international conferences or youth events such as Junior Weekends, or attending congregational weekends at the Nightingale Centre in Great Hucklow. Other activities included supporting Gay Pride marches; membership of a choir, a Bereavement and Loss Support Group, and a covenant group; and visiting Star Island off the coast of New Hampshire to enjoy programmes organised by the Unitarian Universalist Association.

*Unitarians: Together in Diversity*

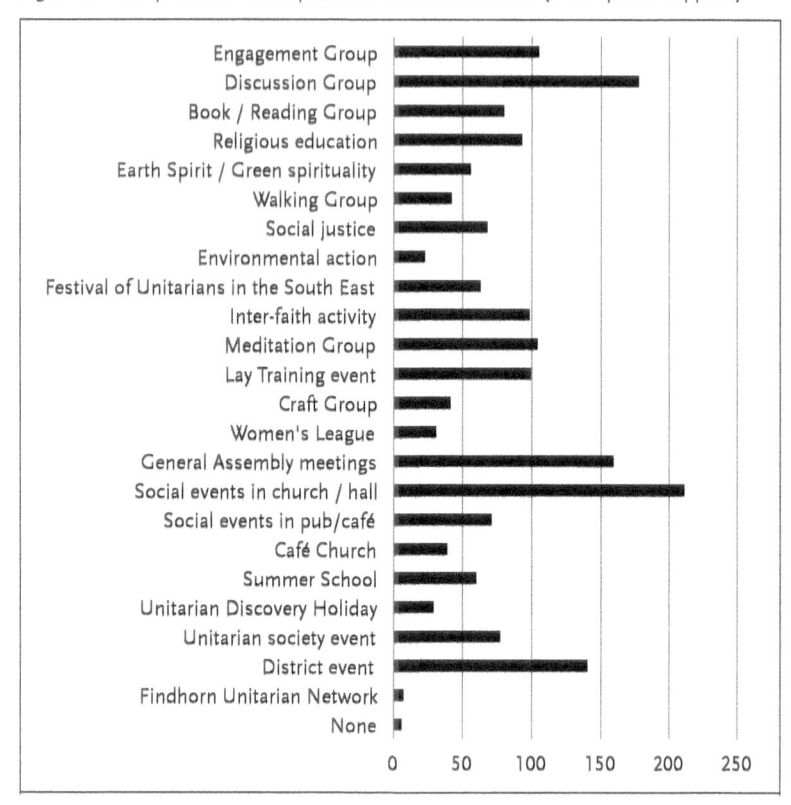

Figure 12.3: Respondents' Participation in Unitarian Activities (from options supplied)

| Activity | Count |
|---|---|
| Engagement Group | ~105 |
| Discussion Group | ~180 |
| Book / Reading Group | ~80 |
| Religious education | ~95 |
| Earth Spirit / Green spirituality | ~55 |
| Walking Group | ~45 |
| Social justice | ~70 |
| Environmental action | ~25 |
| Festival of Unitarians in the South East | ~65 |
| Inter-faith activity | ~100 |
| Meditation Group | ~105 |
| Lay Training event | ~100 |
| Craft Group | ~45 |
| Women's League | ~30 |
| General Assembly meetings | ~160 |
| Social events in church / hall | ~215 |
| Social events in pub/café | ~75 |
| Café Church | ~40 |
| Summer School | ~60 |
| Unitarian Discovery Holiday | ~30 |
| Unitarian society event | ~75 |
| District event | ~140 |
| Findhorn Unitarian Network | ~5 |
| None | ~5 |

Activities mentioned by only one person included membership of the Hibbert Trust;[20] involvement in the Development Skills Training Programme; participation in the Fellowship Initiative Group; training ministers; training for the ministry; Nightingale Centre Open Day; chapel poetry group; contributions to Unitarian periodicals; Wheel of the Year services; ukulele group; drumming group/sound healing; LDPA[21] Council;

---

20  www.thehibberttrust.org.uk/.
21  London & South Eastern District Provincial Assembly.

MOSA[22] conference; fundraising for the Send a Child to Hucklow Fund;[23] attendance at the Lay Persons' Summer School; and peace activities. As always, these levels of participation may have been greater among the respondents, but it was possible to analyse only what they chose to share.

The last question of the survey asked respondents which Unitarian societies, if any, they were a member of. Their responses are shown in Figure 12.4. Three other Unitarian bodies were mentioned by respondents: the Unitarian Animal Welfare Society, the Gaskell Society (by association), and Uni-Coms (Unitarian Communications), each of which was cited by one respondent.

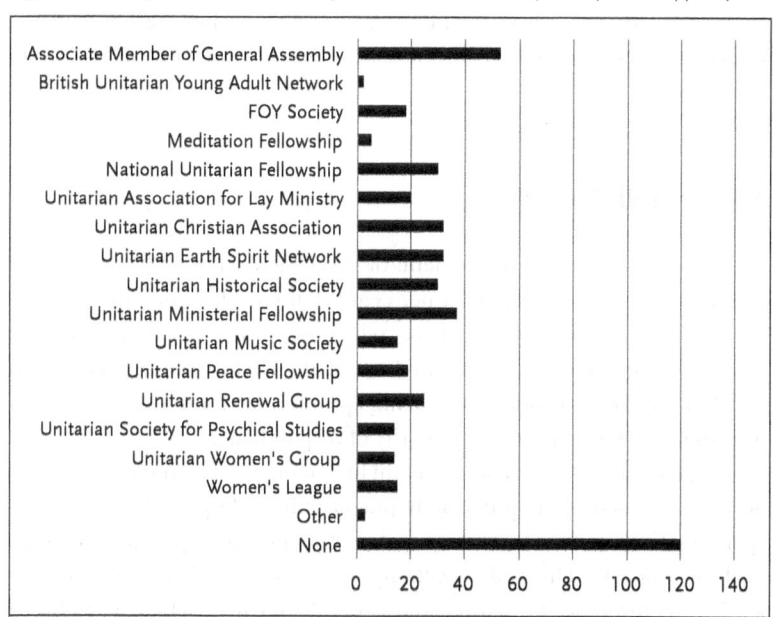

Figure 12.4: Respondents' Membership of Unitarian Societies (from options supplied)

22 Ministerial Old Students' Association.
23 www.sendachildtohucklow.org.uk.

Perhaps the most significant aspect of Figure 12.4 is that 120 respondents (47 per cent, or nearly half) are not members of any Unitarian society. One new Unitarian was unaware that there were so many Unitarian societies in existence, and looked forward to finding out more. The only society to be represented by all the respondents in that category was the Unitarian Ministerial Fellowship, because all ministers and lay pastors automatically become members, although some do not remain in membership.

Again, because the respondents were mainly Unitarian activists, the totals in Figure 12.4, particularly perhaps those for Associate Members of the General Assembly, and also the numbers for members of the Unitarian Association for Lay Ministry and the Unitarian Ministerial Fellowship, may be unrepresentatively high, in comparison with the wider movement. Even so, nearly half of those Unitarian activists were not members of any Unitarian society, a fact which the officers of said societies may wish to reflect on.

## *Summary of findings*

Nearly 60 per cent of the respondents describe themselves as "both religious and spiritual", and a further 24 per cent see themselves as "spiritual, but not religious". Nearly 6 per cent are "religious, but not spiritual", while the remainder (just under 10 per cent) describe themselves as "neither". From which it may be concluded that "being spiritual" is an important aspect of the Unitarian faith of the vast majority of respondents.

Respondents were then asked about their daily, weekly, and less frequent devotional practices. Popular daily practices include prayer; meditation/ spending time in silence; writing and reading practices; physical practices such as yoga, tai chi, reiki, walking, and working on an allotment or gardening; reverence for nature; and gratitude practices. There was a broad range of other practices, which are detailed above. But nearly half of the participants do not have a daily spiritual practice.

This non-participation figure dropped to just over a quarter for weekly spiritual practices, perhaps because many consider attending a Unitarian worship service to be a spiritual practice for them – it was cited by 56 per cent of respondents. There was a wide variety of other practices, which are detailed above. Just over one third of the respondents do not have a less frequent spiritual practice. Those who do cited a whole range of practices, most of which have been mentioned above.

The next question asked about the importance of these practices. More than three-quarters of the respondents find their spiritual practices to be either 'very' or 'fairly' important to them. Only 7 per cent regard them as either 'not very important' or 'not important at all'. This seems very good evidence that the vast majority of Unitarians regard the movement as a body with a spiritual basis and spiritual aims, whatever form they may take.

It is clear from the responses to the four questions about spiritual practices that the respondents have rich and diverse spiritual lives. Yet it is also clear that the numbers declaring that they have no spiritual practice – whether daily (47 per cent), weekly (27 per cent), or less frequent (35 per cent) – do not correspond with the figures given in the first question in this section. There, no fewer than 211 of the 257 respondents (82 per cent) identified themselves as either 'spiritual, but not religious' or 'both religious and spiritual'. This might perhaps be a fruitful area for further study: how Unitarians define what "being spiritual" means in their lives.

The question about participation in Unitarian activities showed that the respondents are actively engaged in the lives of their congregations, and in the wider movement as a whole. As has been acknowledged earlier, the findings reported in this survey are drawn from a very particular Unitarian pool, rather than being necessarily representative of British Unitarians in general. Nevertheless, they do demonstrate the importance of other-than-Sunday activities in the lives of respondents.

The final question asked participants which Unitarian societies they belong to. Perhaps the most significant return was that 120 of them (47 per cent, or nearly half) are not members of any Unitarian society. But once again, because the respondents were mainly Unitarian activists, it is difficult to draw any conclusions from the figures for society membership.

In conclusion, the 257 respondents do not solely attend Unitarian worship on a Sunday (although very many do that also!). Many lead very active spiritual lives, and many also participate enthusiastically in other-than-Sunday activities, whether at a congregational level, or in the wider Unitarian movement.

## *Questions for reflection and group discussion*

1. *Do you have a daily or weekly (or less frequent) spiritual practice?*

2. *If so, how important is it to you?*

3. *Do you take part in Unitarian-led activities (apart from Sunday worship)?*

# Chapter 13
# What holds British Unitarians together in the twenty-first century?

This final chapter seeks to draw some conclusions about what holds Unitarians together as a coherent religious and spiritual community. It will be apparent from the analysis, commentary, and quotes from respondents to the questionnaire that, with regard to belief, there is a very wide range of spiritual and religious positions among contemporary British Unitarians. This was particularly evident in Chapter 7, where, for example, when participants were asked for their views on the importance to them of the Holy Spirit, the two most strongly contrasted options ('Irrelevant to me' and 'Divine spark within') both attracted a significant number of votes. When asked in Chapter 8 about the importance of Christian festivals, participants revealed a similar divergence of opinion, with 41 respondents either declaring them to be of 'no importance' or not answering the question at all, while the remainder found some importance in one or more of the festivals. The 'freedom to believe as their consciences dictate' (to quote the Object of the Unitarian General Assembly) is well exercised.

There were a number of references to spiritual growth as a process, or a journey, and to the principles and values directing that journey. Chapter 2 in particular explored how Unitarians use freedom, reason, and tolerance as ways of measuring and informing the journey. Many respondents to the question about the approach to tolerance, however, did not opt for a single statement, but rather for a combination of two or three statements – notably 'openness to the new' and 'accepting that others do not share our beliefs'. A similarly large majority supported 'the right to work out for themselves what gives their lives meaning' and 'the freedom to question and doubt'. Evidently 'a free and inquiring religion' (to quote the GA Object) is a good description of the way in which Unitarians undertake their spiritual journey. The full text of the General Assembly's Object, revised in 2001, reads as follows:

> *We, the constituent congregations, affiliated societies and individual members, uniting in a spirit of mutual sympathy, co-operation, tolerance and respect; and recognising the worth and dignity of all people and their freedom to believe as their consciences dictate; and believing that truth is best served where the mind and conscience are free, acknowledge that the Object of the Assembly is: To promote a free and inquiring religion through the worship of God and the celebration of life; the service of humanity and respect for all creation; and the upholding of the liberal Christian tradition.*[24]

In practice, 'the worship of God' is not a mandatory requirement for membership of a Unitarian congregation, although it remains an important element for many Unitarians. Chapter 6, exploring Unitarian perspectives on Divinity, revealed a wide range of views on both the descriptive language and the concept itself.

There are words in the GA Object that resonate with many of the comments made by respondents to the questionnaire: *mutual sympathy, co-operation, respect, the worth and dignity of all people* – particularly in Chapter 4, where morality is explored. These are qualities that describe how people should behave and interact in personal relations; and they are the qualities that enable Unitarians to be together in their approach to exploring matters of ultimate value, despite the diversity of their personal beliefs. For many years the General Assembly of Unitarian and Free Christian Churches used in its literature and official statements the phrase *'many beliefs, one faith'*. Like all such phrases, it tends to simplify a more complex set of realities, but it is nonetheless a powerful summary of what Unitarianism is about. An ethos of welcoming a diverse range of beliefs, of offering a supportive community in which to explore religious and spiritual questions, is key to understanding the nature of the Unitarian movement, and it is enshrined in the GA Object.

---

24 General Assembly of Unitarian and Free Christian Churches *The Object*, https://www.unitarian.org.uk/pages/our-object-and-constitution, accessed 27 October 2017.

Accepting that that there is such a diverse range of beliefs among Unitarians, how might it be possible to articulate the commonality of view, approach, and attitude which might be considered to define what it means to be a Unitarian in Great Britain today? The statements which follow are an attempt to draw a list of such commonalities from the answers of the respondents. It is acknowledged that not every statement may speak to all Unitarians with equal force, but perhaps this also says something positive about being a Unitarian.

To be a Unitarian is:
- to acknowledge the primacy of freedom, reason, and tolerance in shaping the religious and spiritual journey
- to accept that freedom, reason, and tolerance do have some limits, and that there are other influences: life experience and a supportive community, for example
- to engage deeply with moral and ethical issues
- to care about the wider world in which one lives, and to strive to put one's ethical and moral values into practice
- to connect respectfully with other faith traditions, and to accept that fellow Unitarians may have different views
- to draw one's own conclusions about the personal significance, if any, of the concept of divinity
- to value dialogue and the exchange of ideas, in community with other Unitarians in worship and other activities
- to have an open heart and an open mind.

These attributes are the reasons why the Unitarian movement holds together, despite the broad diversity of its members' beliefs. Unitarians recognise and cherish the reality that each one of them is on a religious and spiritual journey; that there are no definitive answers to questions of faith and spirituality; and that every person has the right to follow the dictates of his or her own reason and conscience, so long as this does not harm others. Unitarian communities are recognised as supportive contexts in which to inquire and explore, without having to dissimulate, most of the time.

Unitarans welcome diversity of beliefs and together they try to foster an inclusive approach to matters of religious belief and spirituality. There is a high level of tolerance of other beliefs, but more than that: a wholehearted acceptance of them as some of the many factors that enrich and inform their spiritual journey. Their faith has developed into one based on the primacy of individual conscience. They believe that a shared approach to matters of religious belief and spirituality is more important than a statement of shared beliefs, recognising that the spiritual journey is unique to each person.

Readers will have noted at the head of every chapter, except this one, a short quotation from a hymn in a current Unitarian hymnbook, encapsulating the theme of the chapter. Hymns are by nature simple and direct in their expression; there can be no complex theology, and the language and imagery, in the best examples, are simple and have an immediate impact. In some of the chapter-heading verses there are phrases that point to the findings of this conclusion. Unitarians are indeed "people of many kinds" and are urged "in search of truth (to) adventure boldly, and explore". In our searching we acknowledge that "that which for us is Divine" will be found in "what claims our heart and mind". But it is the verse that concludes this final chapter that is summative in its breadth, that speaks of both Unitarian diversity and togetherness, and does so in the context of community:

> *So once more we gather,*
> *Fellowship to share,*
> *Seek an understanding,*
> *Trust with far and near;*
> *And, though ideas differ,*
> *In this thought rejoice:*
> *Love can form from all our*
> *Songs, one song, one voice.*

(Frank R. Clabburn, *Hymns for Living*, 171)

# *Recommendations for further reading*

This reading list includes books about Unitarianism, and about various aspects of Unitarian beliefs and practices, together with some books about spirituality and spiritual practices, most of them also written by Unitarians, or by Unitarian Universalists. The ones marked with an asterisk (*) are out of print but are available as PDFs (see following paragraph). The ones marked with a hash (#) are out of print but available from Amazon as second-hand books.

Many of the older texts may be available in the libraries of Unitarian congregations, or may be accessed online via the Unitarian General Assembly's Document Library at https://www.unitarian.org.uk/resources/document-library/

Alexander, Scott W. (ed.) *Everyday Spiritual Practice: Simple Pathways for Enriching Your Life* (Skinner House Books, 1999).

Buehrens, John A. and Forrest Church *A Chosen Faith: An Introduction to Unitarian Universalism* (Beacon Press, 1998).

Chryssides, George D. (ed.) *Unitarian Perspectives on Contemporary Religious Thought* (Lindsey Press, 1999).

Chryssides George D. (ed.) *Unitarian Perspectives on Contemporary Social Issues* (Lindsey Press, 2003).

Courtney, Cathal *Towards Beloved Community: Finding Hope for Religion & Spirituality in Postmodernity* (Exposure Publishing, 2007) #

Goring, Jeremy and Rosemary Goring *The Unitarians* (Religious and Moral Education Press, 1984) #

Hall, Alfred *Beliefs of a Unitarian*, 3rd edition (Lindsey Press, 1962) *#

Hewett, Phillip *An Unfettered Faith: The Religion of a Unitarian* (Lindsey Press, 1955, reprinted 1958 & 1962) *

Hewett, Phillip *On Being a Unitarian* (Lindsey Press, 1968) *

Hewett, Phillip *The Unitarian Way* (Canadian Unitarian Council, 1985, reissued 2015)

Hostler, John *Unitarianism* (Hibbert Trust, 1981) *

Lingwood, Stephen (ed.) *The Unitarian Life: Voices from the Past and Present* (Lindsey Press, 2008)

Long, Arthur J. *Faith and Understanding: Critical Essays in Christian Doctrine* (Lindsey Press, 1963) *

McLachlan, John *The Divine Image* (Lindsey Press, 1972) *

McLennan, Scotty *Christ for Unitarian Universalists: A New Dialogue with Traditional Christianity* (Skinner House Books, 2016)

Marshall, Vernon *The Larger View: Unitarians and World Religions* (Lindsey Press, 2007)

Parke, David B. (compiler) *The Epic of Unitarianism: Original Writings from the History of Liberal Religion* (Skinner House Books, 1985) #

Reed, Cliff *Unitarian: What's That? Questions and Answers about a Liberal Religious Alternative* (Lindsey Press, 1999; latest edition 2018)

Smith, Leonard *The Unitarians: A Short History* (Blackstone Editions, 2006, 2008)

Smith, Matthew F. (ed.) *Prospects for the Unitarian Movement* (Lindsey Press, 2002) #

Twinn, Kenneth (ed.) *Essays in Unitarian Theology: A Symposium* (Lindsey Press, 1959) *

Usher, David *Life Spirit: for Groups and Individuals Exploring Deep Questions* (Lindsey Press, 2015)

Usher, David *Twelve Steps to Spiritual Health* (Lindsey Press, 2013)

Vest, Norvene and Liz Forney *What is Your Practice? Lifelong Growth in the Spirit* (Morehouse Publishing, 2015)

Whyman, Kate (ed.) *Living with Integrity: Unitarian Values and Beliefs in Practice* (Lindsey Press, 2016)

These titles are just a starting point for those interested in learning more about Unitarianism and Unitarians. There are also periodicals, such as *Faith and Freedom*, a scholarly journal published twice a year; *The Inquirer*, which is the movement's fortnightly magazine; and the periodicals of individual Unitarian societies, such as the Unitarian Christian Association's *The Liberal Christian Herald*, the Unitarian Earth Spirit Network's *The File*, and the National Unitarian Fellowship's *Viewpoints* series, to mention but a few.

# *Acknowledgements*

It would not have been possible to write this book without the help of many people. I would like to thank the following for their input and support:

- Yvonne Aburrow, my good friend, for her help and support, particularly with the online survey.
- Rev. Alex Bradley, my mentor for this project, for the time and trouble he took to read the drafts, and for his wise and insightful comments.
- The members of the Keele Group, who kindly went through the first draft of the questionnaire and suggested many improvements. Any remaining flaws are my own.
- Rev. Ant Howe, for allowing me to stay in his cottage in Trawsfynydd for a week of peace in which to do the data crunching and initial analysis.
- David Dawson and Catherine Robinson, of the Lindsey Press, for their meticulous work on the text.
- Maz, David, and Becky Woolley for their help, encouragement, and support, at all stages of the project.
- The Midland Unitarian Association and Banbury Unitarian Fellowship for their support, and for allowing me to take a sabbatical in which to do the analysis and writing. And all the congregations of the Midland Unitarian Association for their support.
- All the Secretaries of Unitarian congregations in Great Britain who spread the word about the survey, which led to such a good return.
- David Chidgey (artglassmosaics.com) for permission to use his beautiful mosaic on the front cover.

And last, but by no means least, the 257 Unitarians who spent hours filling out the survey forms, for their wonderful insights, and for their enthusiasm and belief in the project. It has been a privilege to be on this journey with you all.

*Sue Woolley*
*December 2017*

# *About the author*

Sue Woolley became a Unitarian at the age of 18, on reading Alfred Hall's *Beliefs of a Unitarian*, which invited her to set off on a faith journey free from dogma and creed. She became a minister in 2011 and serves as District Minister of the Midland Unitarian Association. Her other interests are in training lay worship leaders, and in working for peace.

Printed in August 2021
by Rotomail Italia S.p.A., Vignate (MI) - Italy